LEADING LEARNING IN A CHANGING WORLD

Using Children's Literature for Professional Dialogue

Jacqueline E. Jacobs
Julie A. Rotholz

ScarecrowEducation
Lanham, Maryland • Toronto • Oxford
2005

Published in the United States of America
by ScarecrowEducation
An imprint of The Rowman & Littlefield Publishing Group, Inc.
4501 Forbes Boulevard, Suite 200, Lanham, Maryland 20706
www.scarecroweducation.com

PO Box 317
Oxford
OX2 9RU, UK

British Library Cataloguing in Publication Information Available

Library of Congress Cataloging-in-Publication Data

Jacobs, Jacqueline E., 1947–
  Leading learning in a changing world : using children's literature for professional
dialogue / Jacqueline E. Jacobs Julie A. Rotholz.
    p. cm.
  Includes bibliographical references and index.
  ISBN 1-57886-187-X (pbk. : alk. paper)
  1. Teachers—In-service training. 2. Children's literature—Bibliography. 3.
Children's literature—Study and teaching (Continuing education) I. Rotholz, Julie A.,
1956– II. Title.

LB1731.J23 2005
370'.71'55—dc22

                                                    2004015493

⊗™ The paper used in this publication meets the minimum requirements of
American National Standard for Information Sciences—Permanence of
Paper for Printed Library Materials, ANSI/NISO Z39.48-1992.
Manufactured in the United States of America.

CONTENTS

PREFACE

If you ask a group of teachers to describe their schools, you might get responses like these:

> My school is like a team of untrained mules. We're all pulling the same load, but in different directions.
>
> My school is an octopus quoting the Gospel according to Matthew 6:3: "Do not let your left hand know what your right hand is doing."
>
> My school is an overloaded washing machine. It's often off balance and doesn't get the clothes clean. It's so bad sometimes that it stops altogether.
>
> My school is a candy factory. We deal with sweet little things all day.

Likewise, an administrator might say the following:

> Developing teachers into a collaborative team is like herding cats; everyone is heading to the food dish, but each wants to get there his own way.

Metaphors and similes are useful tools to help us make sense of a complicated world, a world we all wish would make sense. We often turn to metaphors that use a few words to speak volumes. Teachers and administrators understand this. As students (and teachers) of organizational and instructional theory and culture, we understand this, too.

Although its purported topic is professional development, this book is about metaphor. We are, after all, symbolic creatures; we categorize our experiences by their root, by the familiarity of "likes." The understandings we attach to the most mundane and significant categories of our lives are often fashioned into meaning by metaphor or simile. Language itself is metaphor, as words are stand-ins for something else. Much of education is, of course, metaphorical in nature. We create categories, make meaning, and organize our experience from metaphorical beginnings, and it is from such beginnings that we conceptualized this handbook.

Why are children's books so central to this text? They are themselves metaphor, in form, content, and perhaps even delivery. Many among us were lucky to have our first words on a printed page read to us while nestled in a lap belonging to a mother or father, or perhaps a grandparent. From our earliest experiences with the printed word, we have continued to embrace and behold the magic—and the metaphor—that is the children's book. From *Goodnight Moon* to *Pat the Bunny* to *Where the Wild Things Are*, many have learned about the world and our place in it. Beyond the content, as children, we were joined in communion with others because someone read to us. Thus, for the lucky, some of our earliest understandings and attempts at making meaning were cast in someone's lap while our eyes perused the pages of a book. For some of us—including Julie's now seven-year-old son—the first act of obedience was compliance with the simple directive to "turn the page."

The beginnings of this book grew out of Jacque's work with graduate students who were developing their skills and talents in the supervision of instruction. How can one teach about teaching, supervise supervisors about supervision, or model effective methods for professional development presentations if the very essence of our work, teaching children and young people, is lost? A language was found in the rich textures of children's literature, in the metaphors embedded in poetic language. Over time, Julie and another colleague, Diane Harwell, joined forces with Jacque to learn together that the most perplexing of topics (e.g., the effects of poverty, the value of diversity, collisions regarding religion in public schools) could be broached and presented in simple yet profound ways. Over the years, our graduate students used children's literature to present their own lessons to improve schools as places of learning for the students enrolled and the teachers and administrators who lead them. The ideas have been disseminated, but the question was frequently asked, "Do you have a book on this strategy? One where I can just open it up and have the information to tackle a topic I need to discuss within my school?" This handbook is yours to use. We hope it meets your expectations and the challenges you encounter as you continue to push the envelope to improve schooling for children and young people.

Although children's literature is the vehicle for the delivery of programmatic content, the audience for this book is by no means limited to elementary school personnel. The beauty and power of children's literature should not be lost on secondary or even postsecondary professionals and administrators. Indeed, it is the paradox of simplicity and complexity that lends children's literature its power—as well as the effects of the fine art of illustration—to broach topics from a distance, yet draw participants into their message at the same time. Children's literature has proved a sturdy transport for the heaviest messages and an accessible vehicle to help teachers confront painful topics central to the day-to-day life of schools.

The audience for this book is also not limited to facilitators trained in the strategy we propose. This volume provides a step-by-step plan to assist even the novice administrator with the tools to conduct meaningful, relevant professional development sessions, without relying on outside consultants, costly materials, or heavy investments of employee time and energy.

Leading Learning in a Changing World is the first of two volumes on the topic of conducting professional development activities with the help of children's literature. In it we address topics that are often difficult to articulate and sensitive to explore yet undergird the very essence of the human lives that make up schools: students, teachers, administrators, staff, parents, and community members. Some of these topics will be immediately needed in particular schools and others may be "down the road" topics as the adults in the school community find a comfort level with each other in exploring those dilemmas that affect schooling. However uncomfortable we may be with their presence and power in schools, topics such as poverty, death, homosexuality, child abuse, diversity, and disabilities affect us all. Through the use of children's literature as metaphor, we hope to "lower the front step" so that all educators who care about the educational experiences of children and young people can walk out of professional development sessions more confident of their abilities to confront such issues, more skillful in their articulation of the complexities of them, and more committed to continuing a dialogue with their peers about the educational process in all of its complexities.

We hope that committed educators will continue to make meaningful differences in the lives of the students they teach. We offer this handbook as a tool to not simply affect teachers' understandings of social issues and problems, but through them, students' perceptions that school is indeed a caring and humane place. Most of all, we hope to help students and teachers feel understood and valued. Through this handbook, we seek to create a more just and peaceful world, so teachers can say: *My school is a zoo. We have tamed the tiger, marveled at the intelligence of the chimpanzee, and rejoiced in the beauty of the peacock. And we are no longer endangered.*

ACKNOWLEDGMENTS

To the authors and illustrators of children's books, you made this book possible. Your collective genius in the creation of interesting and often challenging topics into such beautifully simple language and artistic illustrations provides the framework to help adults explore issues that are often hard for us to discuss. To our students, who have amazed us by their embrace of this format, enlarged our perspective by your choices of children's literature, and proven that this format works, thank you! We are greatful to Andrew Barbone, Elizabeth Houck, Russ Harless, Joya Gregg, Janet Buzhardt, Cheryl Guy, and Christina Amsterdam, students or graduates in educational leadership at USC, for their support of this work in the development of the cover. Also, we express thanks to Michael Cogdill and Jill K. Cogdill for agreeing to let use their book, *Cracker the Crab and the Sideways Afternoon*, as part of the cover.

Together, we thank Tom Koerner, education editor, for his willingness to listen and to consider that this format of professional development can help our professional colleagues enjoin the dialogue that has the potential to move us forward during unique times in our country. To Cindy Tursman, managing editor, thank you for your patience in working through the many details of putting together a publishable work.

Thanks, also, to Nicole Carty, our production editor, for her thoroughness, good humor, and patience. Your assistance is greatly appreciated.

As coauthors, we each have people without whom we could not have done this work. First, I, Jacque Jacobs, have to thank all the people along the way who have believed in my ability to teach and motivate others to learn and grow: the children and young people I've been privileged to teach and the many adult students and colleagues with whom I've been honored to share learning. To the memory of my mother and father, who taught me the power of education, and to the memory of my late husband, John F. Jacobs, this is but one more testament to the belief you had in me and the unerring belief you had in the innocence and wisdom of children. To Cheri Jacobs, Bonnie Jacobs Coats, Mark Coats, children of mine by our mutual choice, and to Amy Kimball, my daughter regained, I am proud of each of you and thank you for your belief in me. To my grandchildren, Kris, Michael, and Hannah, you continue to inspire me and help me keep my positive belief in all that is good in public education in America. To C. Stanley Lomax, thank you for your continuous support and belief in me. To Julie, a mother through birth and adoption, you are my sister-friend. Thank you for everything

With Jacque, I am grateful to our University of South Carolina graduate students in educational leadership for their enthusiasm and profound desire to make a difference in the struggling, and too often underfunded, public schools of our state. You have rekindled my faith in not only the power of intellectual engagement but in the ever present—though sometimes dimmed—hope for social justice. You, and the students you serve, make our efforts worthwhile.

To Suevann Gentry, first grade teacher extraordinaire, I will always remember and be grateful for your dedication and irrepressible enthusiasm for teaching. You energize and inspire me every time I walk into your classroom. To Aretha Pigford, thank you for your innumerable lessons about race, schools, and professional commitment. As always, I am in awe of you. To Norman and Jewel Rotholz, thanks for your quiet faith in me. To my son, Jonah, who as a baby first complied with my request "to turn the page": Thanks for being every mother's dream. I am so thankful you are mine. To Gracie, my darling daughter: You are a miracle of love incarnate. May you continue to find your own unique voice. There are books in you, too, to be written *and* illustrated. And to my husband, David: You are, now as always, my anchor, my best friend, and my life's unexpected gift. You have made it possible for our home to overflow with not only books but also love.

Finally, this book is testament to the power of collaboration in public education. A simple idea borne of the desire to continue a commitment to make a positive difference for children and young people has grown. To educators everywhere, thank you for *all* that you do every day for the children and young people of the world. Stand up and be heard for the fine educators you are. Be proud of your ability to impart knowledge, no matter how reluctant the learner, and continue to do good work.

INTRODUCTION

I confess! For more than 15 years I have not looked forward to faculty meetings. Over all this time, I've allowed our meetings to fall into the stereotypic pattern dreaded mandated gatherings that jolt us from our teaching day into a 50-minute rapid firing of disconnected announcements and abbreviated discussions about issues that require much more time and thought. (Hebert 1999, p. 219)

PURPOSE

School leaders, as proponents of lifelong learning and witnesses to the need for increasing teachers' expertise, have provided professional development programs, either by their own initiative or by that of district office personnel. Such programs have typically targeted issues related to effective teaching, discipline, or testing strategies; still others have centered on larger professional issues or personal aspects of the teaching profession. Embraced by some as an important vehicle for the continued development of the teaching corps, programs have been similarly scorned as a waste of teachers' time, a "dog and pony show" that benefits only the highly paid consultants who provide the programs, or a needless relic of discarded school reform agendas. Nonetheless, as state and national mandates mount, efforts to identify and address teacher deficiencies, needed structural revisions in the teaching and learning process, and myriad problems of student achievement, efforts to inform and educate, via professional development programs, are bound to continue, if not proliferate. If concerns about the value of in-service programs are legitimate, how can school leaders, desperate to meet or exceed performance demands, provide meaningful and effective professional development programs? We suggest it is critical to start at the school level.

The issue of professional development transcends the simple delivery of content. Certainly, a teaching staff is capable of mastering material. Too often, professional development focuses on improving teachers' technical skills, but not on what they believe and value, and similarly, not on what they are willing to actively change in their personal professional practice. In order to improve professional development activities, the focus must address the "how," or human dimension of delivery, not simply the "what"; hence, the need for this handbook.

At its core, the business of schools is educating every child. Although teacher preparation programs present effective teaching strategies, the realities of new, and even experienced, teachers challenge the adequacies of preservice preparation. Often, the problems faced by teachers, and those that should be targeted by school leaders as likely themes for professional development programs, are those related to coping with the structures of schools and the social realities inherent in American communities, such as poverty and racism. These topics are value-loaded and, too often, are threatening to school staff. Instead of opening up, the individuals most in need of examining the world from a different point of view close down.

Through the innovative use of children's literature, this handbook provides the structure, as well as content, for breaking through the resistance to exploring some of these complex issues. Using children's literature as metaphor, topics such as poverty, peer pressure, and family structures are addressed. Volume 2, *Leading Learning for School Improvement: Using Children's Literature for Professional Dialogue*, addresses such topics as faculty work life, high-stakes testing, and differentiated instruction. The approach is communal; an outcome is personal leadership development.

Unlike most programs that depend on individual interest and commitment, a central tenet of these handbooks is the importance of teamwork and leadership, not simply in the exercises themselves, but as carried through subsequent efforts at school transformation. We see teamwork and leadership as intrinsically linked. Through the focused teamwork inherent in these exercises, school professionals are urged to identify and solve problems at the personal, classroom, and school level. Such teamwork spurs the development of professional relationships. After all, it is only through the efforts of committed professionals who are able and willing to function in a collegial and collaborative manner that real change occurs (Glickman, Gordon, and Ross-Gordon 2003), particularly in high poverty schools (Carter 2000).

Teamwork, as prompted by the exercises in this handbook, enhances shared leadership at the school level. Through collaborative teamwork, site-specific problems are examined in a nonthreatening way. Thus, the goal is not simply a mastery of necessary content to improve faculty performance, but the beginning of an ongoing dialogue, and a commitment to action on issues of central relevance to education at the local level. Insight is easy; purposeful action requires leadership and teamwork.

Because the handbook's primary vehicle for the delivery of these professional development activities is children's literature, by default the focus of the programs remains the same: children. As passionate advocates for children, the authors maintain that the central premise of all professional development activities must be improving the school, home, and community environments of students. Any professional development activity that does not fundamentally benefit students will fall short of what professional development programs should be all about. Even programs that specifically target teacher concerns, such as stress or financial management, have the same goal: to provide the kind of professional and 'glad-to-be-in-this-classroom' teacher that every student deserves.

INTENDED AUDIENCE

This handbook and its companion volume are designed and written for school administrators, consultants, teacher leaders, and other individuals responsible for or interested in meaningful, content rich professional development programs. Although an assumption is often made that the use of children's literature is only appropriate in preschool and elementary school settings, the use of literature as metaphor has wide-ranging applications, particularly at the middle and high school level. This is true not only for middle and secondary level teachers, but for their students. In fact, teachers at such schools will learn valuable instructional strategies that can serve as bridges for addressing complex issues with adolescents such as classism and racism. Certainly the use of children's literature as metaphor is appropriate at such ages, as is the necessity to address many of the topics addressed in these handbooks, particularly those that address value-loaded issues.

Principals and superintendents will find this a valuable resource, not simply as a tool for fostering faculty development, but also for any staff member responsible for mentoring and modeling appropriate teaching behaviors (Huling and Resta 2001). This is certainly true as differentiated instruction assumes center stage (Tomlinson 2001). Professional development is, at its heart, teaching; teaching should always begin with the learner. Each handbook may, therefore, serve as a reminder to those at the highest organizational levels how numerous and complex are the topics that teachers face every day. It is a resource that we hope will encourage administrators to address sensitive and controversial topics that are often overlooked, such as child abuse, religion in public schools, or affectional orientation.

Each handbook is also useful for college and university faculty members who prepare preservice teachers, and in graduate programs, such as educational leadership or counselor education. The handbooks may be particularly useful in courses on the supervision of instruction, as they provide a framework to address professional development needs in a nonthreatening, supportive, and creative manner. The handbook "models," in both form and content, the very behaviors needed for effective supervision. Each topic is supported by background materials, relevant professional literature, and recommended readings. Furthermore, the format used in each handbook takes learners from their current position or level of expertise and gently guides them toward a richer and fuller understanding of the topic. Each section includes not simply suggestions for further reading, but suggestions for moving "from insight to purposive action," thus translating ideas into effective educational practice.

HOW IS THIS HANDBOOK DIFFERENT FROM OTHERS?

The use of metaphor, specifically the centrality of children's literature, is pivotal to the power and appeal of this handbook. Children's literature is, almost by nature, nonthreatening. Easy to understand and appreciate, children's books can help adults to address, from a seemingly simplistic perspective, complex issues. Our argument is that the innocence inherent in children's books often masks these books' power and metaphorical allure. Paradoxically, their simplicity makes them rich; their metaphorical use can be both sharp and obtuse.

All of the exercises in this handbook start with an exploration of the learner's knowledge of, and stake in, the content. Before information is presented, a Setting the Stage activity requires individuals to take a position on an issue. At the very outset, participants have an investment in the discussion's outcome, process, and resolution. The format provides the needed structure to ensure the goals of the program are met, but also allows for the modification of content to address specific needs. Discussion questions are provided, as well as information for the facilitator. In addition, each handbook provides examples of how to address emotional and value-loaded topics—a concern of virtually every school leader in America. The format is user-friendly; the supportive structure of this handbook provides a comprehensive how-to from start to finish.

CHAPTER FORMAT

Following the introduction, an orientation outlines the book's content and background. The next three chapters address an overarching category, beginning with background information and an overview of why the category is important in contemporary society and its value as a topic for professional development. Although each topic is distinct, the topics share some commonalities. These commonalities are evident in the supporting literature that grounds the sets of activities. Recommended readings are provided for each literature selection. Finally, appendix C provides formatted but blank pages for revisions and additions. The authors' intent is that this handbook be a work in progress for the user. Blank pages indicate that the readers can design their own professional development activities; we provide the encouragement and the format to do just that.

The introduction and chapter 1 provide an orientation, as well as overview and background to the thematic categories. The discussion in chapters 2–4 is presented in the following how-to steps:

Purpose: At a glance, the reader can determine if the suggested activity will address one of the school's professional development priorities.

Materials: Details about the children's book, including a complete citation (with ISBN), are provided. Any needed supplemental materials are listed. Supplemental materials may include a flip chart, an overhead projector, computer projector, or arts and crafts supplies. Depending on the size of the group, a microphone and speakers may be necessary as well.

Abstract of the children's book: A brief description of the storyline is presented, as not all readers will be familiar with this genre's literature. The intent of this brief "snapshot" is to place the subsequent steps into a proper context and to begin to forge a metaphorical link between the text and the purpose of the activity. The metaphorical use of the story is then briefly explained. Please note: The original children's book text is *required* for each individual program. The intent is that the story is read aloud, usually word for word, and its illustrations shared. This is the vital link to connect the Setting the Stage activity to the insights that follow. The abstract is included only to inform the facilitator of the type of text used in the activity.

Setting the stage: This step requires active engagement in the professional development program. For example, through teamwork or self-reflection, each participant is required to stake a position, share an experience, or analyze a situation. This anticipatory set's goal is to foster self-examination and honesty; this activity may or may not be shared with the large group. Thus, from the outset, participants are doing, not merely listening. Participants thus become architects of their own learning and committed to the unfolding of their experience instead of sitting as passive consumers of a prepackaged "professional develop-ment product."

Notes on reading the book: This section provides additional interpre-tations, alternative activities, or cautionary notes. Additional questions for the facilitator, such as whether the anticipatory set should be shared, who might be the best choice to read the text aloud, or concerns about how to group participants, are posed here. Background information deemed important to fully use the recommended text is also included.

Discussion questions: Following the reading of the book, discussion questions are presented to stimulate contributions from participants, to foster teamwork and collaboration, and to serve as a guide for the facil-itator. These questions help the facilitator and the participants to ana-lyze and understand the Setting the Stage activity conducted previously. Responses to the recommended questions are thus a diagnostic tool for self-exploration, a springboard for the mastery of content, and the groundwork for the integration of new insights.

Facilitating the discussion: Information for the facilitator is provided for the discussion questions. This ensures that the facilitator can lead the discussion and help participants move to purposive action.

Other metaphorical uses or parallels: This section describes multiple metaphors that may be interpreted from the particular children's book. In some instances, specific metaphors are suggested, or other topics for which this book may be used are noted. We have found that a simple children's book may be useful in varied contexts to address multiple is-sues germane to schools and schooling.

Illustrations: This section contains a brief description of the illustra-tions in the book, as well as suggested illustrations of particular note or importance. It is assumed that many of these books will be unfamiliar to most readers.

Recommended background reading: In order to assist the facilitator who may need more information to feel confident in facilitating a dis-cussion on the topic, some specific literature is noted here. The facilita-tor may choose to read more widely, but the references will give a basic framework for the topic.

Insight into action: This section links the learning gleaned from the professional development activity to concrete actions that will bolster student achievement. Instead of simply stopping once conclusions are drawn or new material mastered, this step offers exemplars of what teachers can actually *do* to translate the learning from the just-completed activity to school improvement and, ultimately, student achievement.

Following the three thematic chapters, this volume concludes with the question, "Where do we go from here?" Our first response addresses the issue of program evaluation. Professional development is ongoing and therefore evaluation efforts should be formative, rather than summative, in intent. Acknowledging the positive effects from professional development efforts is pivotal. Similarly, problems or shortcomings must be addressed and remedied when possible. The evaluation strategy, like our strategy for professional development, is developmental and ongoing.

Our second answer to the question, "Where do we go from here?" centers on the development of new professional development programs to address emerging needs within the school community. The central thesis of the final part of the last section is the cyclical nature of program evaluation, modification, and delivery. Our aim is the continuous improvement of school personnel to effect positive change and growth in individual students, as well as the development of the school as a learning community.

THE NEED FOR THIS HANDBOOK

Skepticism may accompany the notion of combining children's literature and professional development. To the cynics, we say that the greatest truths often arrive in the most innocuous of packages. Children's literature, as a vehicle to begin professional development activities, has many advantages: it's often humorous, nonthreatening, aesthetically appealing, and easy to understand. The paradox is that children's literature often addresses issues of grave importance, touches people "where they live," challenges established aesthetics, and is intellectually rich. It is the richness—indeed the paradox—of children's literature that makes it an ideal vehicle to speak to issues of school reform, social quagmires, and contemporary educational dilemmas. Children's books can shine a light on the five-hundred-pound gorilla in the classroom. Teachers will often say, "We do the work but we don't talk about these issues." Children's literature can construct a bridge to dialogue and understanding not only the gorilla but how he got into the classroom in the first place.

The act of teaching in kindergarten through twelfth grade is the transformation of children into adults. Through these professional development exercises, we ask that the adults responsible for this transformation return, albeit briefly, to childhood. It all seems paradoxical: We laugh at children's literature, yet we know it can address the greatest taboo, death. We see children's literature as low-cost entertainment, yet it can illuminate our deepest fears and ugliest self-portraits. We label children's literature as academically vacuous, yet it can address metaphysical truths and pose unanswered—and unanswerable—questions. We read this genre quickly—so few words—yet its illustrations demand that we linger. We let these books languish in the neglected corners of our houses, assuming we are too old for them, yet their timeless quality can touch and inform us in unforeseen ways. We are using children's books, a medium as underrated, magical, and limitless as the audience for whom they were originally written. This is not paradox but a great cyclical congruence.

The teaching of teachers must take center stage if teachers are to meet the challenges of teaching each student. Likewise, the mandates set for them by the federal government, state departments of education, and local communities require dialogue that has not generally been central to what is done in faculty meetings or typical professional development programs. Whether teachers are taught by fellow teachers, school administrators, university faculty, or paid consultants, they must be able to translate their learning into tangible benefits for students. This guide is equally useful for any trainer. Its format lets the facilitator "hit the ground running" in the delivery of content and allows school personnel to deliver professional development, demonstrating that administrators or teacher leaders can do worthwhile professional development in their own environments. Teachers are thus encouraged to assume leadership and ownership of the programs; teamwork is the precursor. The format is value neutral; the activities are not.

The format of the handbook offers more than sound bites for school improvement. The use of children's literature draws on metaphor, art, and "multiple intelligences" to make sense of this tumultuous time in our society. The translation of the children's text to the recommended format demands that participants become actively involved in their own learning. They are producers of meaning, not simply consumers of content.

Finally, we believe that learning ought to be (although it isn't always) fun. Take a survey of classroom teachers and you will learn that professional development programs are seldom, if ever, fun. We set out to change that. Teachers who work with kids all day have better things to do than to sit passively while a talking head preaches to them about what they woulda-coulda-shoulda done in their classrooms. Life is short. Teaching is important. Our aim is to do all we can to make classrooms better places for *all* students. To that end, we offer this handbook. After all, as Goodlad (1984) noted, "We will only begin to get evidence of the potential power of pedagogy when we dare to risk and support markedly deviant classroom procedures" (249).

General guidelines for this type of professional development include the following:

Step 1: Getting ready (two or more days)
> Prepare Setting the Stage items on overheads or for a PowerPoint presentation.
> Prepare Discussion Questions on overheads or for PowerPoint presentation.
> Plan to give out the Setting the Stage sheet at the beginning of the professional development. Do not give out the Discussion Questions until after you have read the book to the participants.
> Read the book a day or more before the session in order to think through the ideas yourself.
> Consider the use of the illustrations from the children's book for the size of the group you have. If you are going to use the illustrations in your PowerPoint, please read the following cautionary notes.

Step 2: During the professional development
> Have the Setting the Stage items visible when people enter the room and set the expectation that they will address them upon entry. The first time you do this you will need to make sure there is paper and pencil for each person. You will need to tell them

whether or not you are going to collect this information (usually you will not), but in either case you want them to write out their answers before you start.

Move around when reading the book so that you are modeling good instructional techniques. While everyone may not be able to see the pictures at the time you read it, assure them that you will pass the book around for them to appreciate the illustrations after it has been read.

Any number of techniques may be used when addressing the Discussion Questions. The authors have found the following to be most successful. Start by having everyone write their own answer. Then you can have participants discuss the question in small groups with each group writing its collective ideas so that they can be gathered, typed as one document, and later disseminated. This step is important so that everyone knows that their ideas are valued and considered. When appropriate, encourage the groups to come to some consensus that they can share with the whole group. It may be that they will need to present several responses to represent the whole group's thinking adequately. Write each of the ideas from the small groups on chart paper or overheads so that all of the groups can see the responses. Focus the discussion of the last question on how, in your setting, you can take the ideas you have generated and move them to positive action.

CAUTIONARY NOTES

As these exercises were field tested, several potential problems emerged. The first is that many of the children's books that we recommend are not paginated. Thus, in describing pages or passages to emphasize, we've had to describe their location in the book or reference it by content or illustration. In some cases we have counted pages from the title page to the relevant passage or illustration.

Second, for large groups, participants may strain to see the illustrations. In such cases, multiple copies of the text may be used, each in a different location. Another option is to project the images on an overhead projector (or use PowerPoint). Some books do have an accompanying CD, which will provide you the illustrations. If you are going to photograph the illustrations, please make sure that you are in compliance with current copyright law for the use of such photographs. Please note that the use of specific technology should have a trial run before the program begins.

Third, these activities should take no more than an hour, and many of them can be less than that, but you must consider the need to monitor the productivity of the discussion. Clearly, some topics and questions will spur heated discussion or contemplation. It is imperative that the facilitator provide a venue for continued dialogue and exploration beyond the initial discussion. Suggestions are provided in chapter 5 of this text for ways to stimulate new learning and applications.

As proponents of lifelong learning, providing the extended venues for follow up and action from the initial discussion ensures that the facilitator is modeling what all teachers want for all learners: Consider, discuss, and grow in knowledge.

● I

THEMATIC CATEGORIES

OVERVIEW AND BACKGROUND

This volume (as the first volume in a projected two-volume set) addresses the value-laden subtexts that touch many aspects of education in America. In the following chapters, we address three categories of issues: the *social realities* (chapter 2) of contemporary life, myriad topics regarding *diversity* (chapter 3), and a host of what we call *community conundrums* (chapter 4)—topics that affect teachers' and students' lives and, by extension, their experience in school. Within the three thematic categories are examples of children's literature that serve as metaphors to address individual topics. For each topic, activities based on at least three different children's books are presented.

The topics covered in this handbook include contemporary issues, as well as perennially problematic issues inherent in education. Classism, racism, and the challenges posed by diverse communities of learners existed long before the founding days of public education. Topics that are more familiar in the day-to-day operations of schools are covered in the second volume: *Leading Learning for School Improvement: Using Children's Literature for Professional Dialogue*. These topics may be less threatening and easier for first-time users of this professional development format. *Leading Learning in a Changing World: Using Children's Literature for Professional Dialogue* is being published first because little professional development material is currently available to address such topics as affectional orientation, religion in public education, and the effects of economic uncertainties on students and teachers. These are difficult topics on which to focus professional development efforts. The reluctance to speak of them candidly prompts our sense of urgency to stimulate conversations about them. Simply because many are hesitant to address such challenges as death, divorce, or developmental disabilities, we are not granted immunity from their effects nor are the students for whom such realities are a constant companion.

Unlike single-topic texts for professional development, this handbook provides rich exemplars to address myriad issues. Because the format is standardized, future professional development programs could be easily melded into it; blank format pages are included in appendix C to encourage the development of idiosyncratic programs. The opportunities to develop additional professional development programs, using this handbook as a model, are limitless.

Chapter 5 includes suggestions for assessing and evaluating the efficacy of these, as well as self-authored, programs. The evaluative chapter emphasizes long-term effects rather than immediate satisfaction, as well as suggesting strategies that are doable within a school setting. An important question is not simply, "Did you like this program?" but, "To what extent did this program affect your professional practice?" "How can these insights translate to positive action?" Chapter 5 concludes with cautionary notes regarding the development of additional programs, including book selection, audience, and suggestions for effective delivery.

We welcome your perusal of these pages and encourage your suggestions to this dialogue on important topics. Since this is a handbook, it is your workbook; make notations about what works and what doesn't and let us know. Involve your faculty or other participants in the selection of needed programs. Above all, be fearless. Our aim, after all, is to improve schools and schooling, since each of us must cope in a changing world. Yours is a great calling. Begin.

THEMATIC CATEGORIES AND TOPICS

2

SOCIAL REALITIES

OVERVIEW AND BACKGROUND

Our nation's schools are struggling. Conservative pundits have noted that the world's largest budget devoted to public education is failing American schools (Pelifian 2002). Given the level of resources devoted to public education, how can our schools continually fail? Professionals at every level of education, however, are quick to note that the tribulations faced by teachers have never been greater. The problems are not simply related to resources, fiscal or human, but are indicative of the inherent problems of American society: family instability, substance abuse, and the effects of a media-saturated culture. If schools are struggling, it is because society is struggling, for schools reflect the communities in which they reside.

Because teachers are taught the mechanics of curriculum construction, classroom management, and assessment techniques to gauge student mastery of material in their preservice teacher education programs, the focus of professional development has been, as it should be, on the technical core of schools: that is teaching and learning. The mission of virtually every school in this country is to develop students' basic competencies to be contributing members of a democratic society. We talk about developing lifelong learners, good citizens, and a technologically literate workforce. What we seldom talk about is the ever-present despair, emotional turmoil, and insecurity that are packed into many students' backpacks. Because these issues are talked about only in subdued voices in the teachers' lounge (if at all), schoolwide conversations and strategies to address them are missing. The topics in this handbook attempt to give form and substance to these closet conversations. After all, it is only when we acknowledge and recognize these issues for what they are (problems that can derail a student's entire educational experience) that we have a chance for constructive intervention.

Numerous issues in American society affect the day-to-day lives of teachers and students. The social realities that educators face with regard to the needs of students include substance abuse, harassment and bullying, values exploration, societal trauma, the weight of poverty, classism, death, divorce, loss, and child abuse and neglect.

A social reality that continues to touch many American families is *substance dependence and abuse*. The majority of the population (61 percent) between eighteen and twenty-five drinks alcohol, 54 percent of those twenty-six and over (Office of Applied Statistics, SAMHSA 2004). Sadly, almost 5 million adults are alcohol dependent or alcohol abusing *and* have at least one child younger than fifteen living at home. More than one-quarter of those parents also use marijuana (National Survey on Drug Use and Health 2002). Clearly many students in our schools are affected in some way by adult chemical abuse.

Sadly, drug and alcohol abuse is a factor, not simply for students who live with an addicted parent. In the 1990s, according to one study, approximately 33 percent of high school seniors reported being drunk at least once in the previous month. Twenty percent of high school sophomores and seniors reported using marijuana in the same period (Schlozman 2002c).

The responsibilities of educators in meeting the needs of students relative to substance abuse range from programs like Drug Abuse Resistance Education (DARE), which is available in most elementary schools in this country, to science classes or daily living classes for middle and high school students, which address the effects of abuse of alcohol, tobacco, and drugs. However, few opportunities exist for educators to discuss their perceptions and understandings about substance abuse and the effects it has on their teaching, student learning, and the emotional needs of students who live in homes where these substances are abused. The activities in this section are designed to provide a vehicle for educators to have this discussion and to consider their own views and needs relative to the educational environment.

We live in a cruel world; unfortunately, some of that cruelty is reflected in the conduct of children. For children and youth who have not had the experience of having their needs met, an available outlet to mask the pain is often cruelty to others. Extremes of *harassment and bullying*, such as gang activity, are on the rise and there appears to be an increase in the incidence of these behaviors on school grounds. According to Klein (1997), more than 261 cities have defined gangs, thus providing the opportunity for boys and girls to seek membership for the sense of meaning and importance that gangs reportedly provide. On a lesser scale, the petty cruelties and ostracism that often characterize behavioral tendencies of school-age children continue to trouble teachers and school administrators. Harassment and bullying are not gender neutral; educators need to be aware that these actions are often used as a way to exclude. Some educators do not believe that they should be concerned about these incidents and others see some of these acts as "part of growing up." Yet the effects on a student's confidence and feelings of safety at school are not to be taken lightly. Helping educators to explore their own perceptions of harassment and bullying and the frequency and intensity with which it occurs within their school can lead to awareness of the responsibilities incumbent on educators to ensure that each student has a safe and orderly environment in which to learn.

Values exploration was chosen to address those aspects of a student's life that are part of what she or he brings to school as family or neighborhood values. Values are developed by the many influences on one's life. The primary unit for development from many is generally the family. How the family identifies personal and social values is influenced by religious beliefs, life experiences, and interactions with others. Often these beliefs are common to the majority in a school and where most share common values. However, as the society becomes more mobile and the changing work place forces adults to seek new life opportunities, the values of the family unit may be challenged and may even change. The focus of this section is to help educators examine their own values and their ability to accept the values of others.

While *societal traumas* have always been a part of our nation's history, the reality of events like September 11, 2001, the shootings at Columbine High School, and the tragedies that daily affect local communities from such things as storms, fires, and random acts of violence make clear that educators must engage in dialogue about the effects of these events on the day-to-day lives of all the members of a school community. The advantage to having discussions before a trauma occurs is that educators, as leaders in a community, will be better prepared to assist others, from the school level to the community at large.

The *weight of poverty* has received a great deal of attention in educational literature in the last decade and is particularly addressed relative to student achievement. In many states, the correlation between poverty and racial minorities is so high that getting the larger community to consider the impact of poverty on learning is obfuscated by preconceived notions about race. The purpose of these activities is to help educators participate in discussions that will consider how poverty affects student learning, determine what their own beliefs and ideas are about the impact of poverty, and consider that even in families of poverty, parents have dreams for their children.

In the democracy that exists in the United States, it is often difficult for educators to accept that there are still class lines. Those class lines may be more blurred than they were in the early 1900s with less emphasis on "blue bloods" as a measure of one's status in the society. There is no question, however, that economic conditions often provide a basis for *classism* that is rarely discussed or considered when trying to determine what is necessary to ensure student success and achievement. The activities in this section are designed to help educators participate in discussions that will assess the effects of classism within their communities and schools.

Death, divorce, and loss affect students and teachers every day. Death comes to family members, friends, and even classmates or teachers. Divorce continues to affect the lives of many students in our schools, whether it occurs while a student is in school or as the issues surrounding divorce continue to challenge the student. Likewise, loss can come in many forms. It may occur for a student who has to move away from your school or community and realizes that he or she will leave behind friends and familiar surroundings. It may occur in the obverse for students who are new to your school after leaving familiar surroundings in another place. The importance of discussions among educators on issues of death, divorce, and loss lie in their preparedness to consider the effects of these life events on student emotions, actions, and achievement.

The final topic in this section relates to *child abuse and neglect*. Most educators are aware of students who have been abused or neglected, but often are not sure what they can or should do. Sometimes just the recognition of the signs of child abuse and neglect is sufficient to refer the student for help. But, sometimes educators who may have little exposure or experience with child abuse and neglect need to engage in dialogue with other educators about what they can do, how they can be of assistance, and when or how they can ensure that students who are victims of child abuse or neglect can maintain their academic opportunities while coping in a difficult situation.

As student populations change, teachers are often ill prepared to address the needs of students who live in situations such as abuse or neglect, poverty, or where they are victims of harassment or bullying. Yet school is the common denominator for all students in the society. Clearly, the more considerations teachers have given to what they can do and how they will react when faced with these *social realities*, the more likely they will be to experience success in meeting these issues head-on, to maintain calm, and to engage in constructive action. The activities in this chapter are designed to engage educators in dialogue and to help them consider the needs of their individual school communities as they function in an ever changing society and increasingly challenging world.

TOPICS AND BOOKS DISCUSSED IN CHAPTER 2

Substance abuse, 11–17
The Red Ribbon
I Wish Daddy Didn't Drink So Much
The Z Was Zapped
Harassment and bullying, 18–25
Don't Laugh at Me
Wings
Nobody Knew What to Do: A Story about Bullying

SUBSTANCE ABUSE: ACTIVITY 1

Purpose

The purpose of this activity is to explore the risk factors and effects of substance abuse on students and their parents and to determine if there is a way to help students find hope without the use of drugs.

Materials

- Book: J. Lasne, *The Red Ribbon* (Miami, FL: National Family Partnership, 1994). ISBN 0-9642815-0-3
- Red ribbon (enough to have all the participants hold and pass on)
- Chart paper
- Markers

Abstract of the Children's Book

The book shares the lovely tale of the king whose kingdom is in the depths of despair and he does not know what to do about it. After trying to find the wisest people to solve the problem, he finds that the town weaver has the "magic" answer in a long red ribbon.

Setting the Stage

1. Was there a time when you realized that you needed another person or could be the strength for another person? Write a paragraph describing your experience.
2. Think of a time when you needed someone to believe in you and your ability to accomplish something. What were the most important things about that belief and who held those beliefs?

Notes on Reading the Book

The book takes about eight minutes to read, but could also be told beautifully as a folk tale by a good storyteller. The importance of voice is to show the effects of the ribbon when people realize that they are together, or must be together, to find ways to solve problems. Give a strong voice to the weaver and strengthen the king's voice as he becomes aware of the power of each person's belief that she or he could make a positive difference in the lives of others.

Discussion Questions

1. Why has the red ribbon become symbolic of the fight against drugs and substance abuse?

2. How does a student's success in school positively or negatively affect the likelihood of the student using drugs or alcohol?
3. Is the effort to stop substance abuse in schools just addressed during Red Ribbon Week, or is there a conscientious ongoing effort? What does it look like?

Facilitating the Discussion*

1. As depicted in the story, the red ribbon is a symbol of hope that together people can make a positive difference in the lives of others. Elicit comments and reinforce the idea that teamwork is a strong deterrent to substance abuse.
2. Ask teachers to think about evidence that they have where students have avoided drugs or alcohol because they were actively engaged in academics and/or athletics. What can be done to try to engage more students so that they have positive reasons to avoid the use of alcohol or drugs?
3. Ask participants to brainstorm, and record on chart paper, efforts made in your school to help students avoid drugs and alcohol. If the only concerted effort is during Red Ribbon Week, brainstorm things that can be done on an ongoing basis to address the abuse of drugs and alcohol.

*Prior to the group's discussion, ask participants to pass the red ribbon around so that each person is holding it. Then ask the group to look around and see that they are "connected," even as the ribbon twists and turns.

Other Metaphorical Uses or Parallels

The book could be used to discuss the effects of poverty and despair or to address the collaboration between cultures as depicted by the people of different races working together.

Illustrations

The illustrations are colorful and the king is clearly sad (wide mouth, down turned) and ultimately becomes happy because he sees the effects of people working together.

Recommended Background Reading

American Psychiatric Association, "Let's Talk Facts about . . . Substance Abuse and Addiction" (2004). www.psych.org/public_info/substance.cfm.

Insight into Action

If there is not currently a plan in the school to address substance abuse at a time other than Red Ribbon week, determine ways that your faculty and staff can continuously support students, faculty, and staff in being "substance free." Determine ways that the message can be clearly conveyed and provide support for students who have questions about ways to avoid the temptation of drugs or alcohol and/or to recoup from having made the mistakes of abuse. Resources must be available for students who have to cope with parents or caregivers who misuse drugs or alcohol.

SUBSTANCE ABUSE: ACTIVITY 2

Purpose

The purpose of this activity is to help teachers understand the conflicting feelings and the effects those emotions have on children who live with an alcoholic parent.

Materials

- Book: J. Vigna, *I Wish Daddy Didn't Drink So Much* (Morton Grove, IL: Albert Whitman, 1988). ISBN 0-8075-3526-5
- 5×8 lined index cards
- Notebook paper
- Pens or pencils

Abstract of the Children's Book

At Christmastime, Lisa (the story's narrator) expresses hopefulness, anger, and despair about her father's drinking. Despite his gift of a blue

sled he built himself, what Lisa wants most is his company and his ful-
fillment of a promise to go sledding with her. When her father again dis-
appoints her, Lisa struggles to find solace.

Setting the Stage

On the 5×8 index card that you have been given, write a brief paragraph about someone you know who has (or you suspect has) a drinking problem. Do not put your name or any identifying information on
the card.

Notes on Reading the Book

Because substance abuse is a difficult topic, select a reader who has
the sensitivity to give the reading of this book the seriousness it deserves. It's important to allow short periods of silence between particularly moving or sensitive parts of the book. (For example, "I wish just
once, we could have a real Christmas like other people.")

Discussion Questions

1. Were you uncomfortable or ambivalent about writing on your index card, even though you knew no one would see it?
2. Did it cross your mind that someone might see it?
3. Did you think about someone close to you, but then search your
   mind for another example, one that isn't so "loaded" for you?
4. Why does this topic of alcohol abuse garner such strong reactions
   from all of us?
5. Did you or someone who is sitting near you seem to have a hard
   time taking this exercise seriously? Why do you suppose that is?

Facilitating the Discussion

Some staff members may make light of this topic; some adults do not
view "drinking too much" as a "big deal." Perhaps their efforts to make
fun of this topic are a way to mask or deny their own pain with alcohol
and/or an alcoholic family member.

Illustrations

The illustrations capture the emotional distance between Lisa's father and other family members. It may be helpful to ask participants to analyze the sentiments and emotions that are evident in the illustrations. The story itself is powerful; be careful not to neglect the contributions to the storytelling lent by the illustrations.

Recommended Background Reading

Al-Anon Family Group Headquarters, Inc., P.O. Box 862, Midtown Station, New York, NY 10018 (212-302-7240). Children of Alcoholics Foundation, Inc., 555 Madison Ave., 4th floor, New York, NY 10022 (212-754-0656). National Council on Alcoholism, 12 West 21st St., New York, NY 10010 (212-206-6770).

S. C. Schlozman, "The Shrink in the Classroom: When 'Just Say No' Isn't Enough," *Educational Leadership* 59, no. 7: (2002c): 87–89.

Insight into Action

What resources are available in your community for families who are struggling to cope with alcoholism? Is a list of these resources readily available to students and their families? How do families contact such resources? Think of ways, in your community, such resources can be accessed with privacy and dignity.

SUBSTANCE ABUSE: ACTIVITY 3

Purpose

The purpose of this activity is for participants to discuss the many ways that substance abuse can affect students, teachers, and families.

Materials

- Book: C. V. Allsburg, *The Z Was Zapped* (Boston: Houghton Mifflin, 1987). ISBN 0-395-44612-0

Abstract of the Children's Book

This alphabet book provides a poignant descriptor for each letter. The book demonstrates how such a simple thing as the alphabet can be used to express the impact of painful and destructive actions.

Setting the Stage

1. For the letters A, B, and C write a short sentence that describes a negative effect of substance abuse on the lives of a student or teacher. For example, "D" Drug induced state.
2. Can the effects of substance abuse be apparent in a classroom, whether on the part of a student or parent?

Notes on Reading the Book

The book is stark in its use of black and white illustrations and short, cryptic expressions of destruction and gloom. The expression for each letter should be read with a somber voice that reduces the image that many teachers have of the alphabet (e.g., the alphabet song) as an expression of gaiety.

Discussion Questions

1. Think about your descriptors for the letters A, B, and C. How similar were they to those of the author of this book?
2. In what ways could you use some symbol (alphabet, numbers) in your subject area or grade level to help students identify the effects of drug and alcohol abuse in our society?
3. Discuss ways in which faculty takes a proactive stance on the negative effects of drug and alcohol abuse.

Facilitating the Discussion

1. Ask participants to pair/share their own descriptors and then compare to those of the author.
2. Place participants in grade-alike or subject-alike groups (or you might decide to have them work across the curriculum) to brainstorm ways

that they could consider the impact of substance abuse on their subject area. For example, science teachers might have students in high school identify the symbols from the periodic table for different substances that are known to be abused in the surrounding community.

3. Often educators turn a blind eye to the amount of substance abuse present in the lives of their students. Whether the abuse is by the students themselves (e.g., alcohol) or by others in their lives, students are affected. Teachers' efforts to help them relate their learning to these effects are important.

Other Metaphorical Uses or Parallels

This book could also be used to discuss societal traumas or child abuse and neglect.

Illustrations

The illustrations in this book are stark drawings in shades of black, white, and gray. They are evocative of the destruction that surrounds the letter and provide a strong visual for the language that is used to describe the destruction.

Recommended Background Reading

S. C. Schlozman, "The Shrink in the Classroom: Why 'Just Say No' Isn't Enough," *Educational Leadership* 59, no. 7 (2002c): 87–89.

Insight into Action

Although teachers are not generally trained, nor is it necessarily appropriate for them, to counsel students who are substance abusers or who live in an environment with substance abuse, they should certainly be prepared to identify the effects and refer students to the appropriate source for assistance. Follow up this professional development with training on what to look for in student behavior related to substance abuse.

HARASSMENT AND BULLYING: ACTIVITY I

Purpose

The purpose of this activity is to help participants explore the unique abilities, features, and personalities that students, staff, and parents bring to the schooling environment and the challenges that must be addressed to stop harassment in all its forms.

Materials

- Book: S. Seskin and A. Shamblin, *Don't Laugh at Me* (Berkeley, CA: Ten Speed, 2002). ISBN 1-5824605-8-2

Abstract of the Children's Book

This beautiful book illustrates the similarities and differences that all humans share and exhorts us not to "laugh" at one another just because we look or act differently.

Setting the Stage

1. Think of a time when you had to explain to someone else why another individual appeared to be different, in looks or actions, from others.
2. Do you find it difficult to accept a parent who comes to see you when that parent has a disability, either visible or in understanding, or looks "different" from your adult friends?

Notes on Reading the Book

Read the book with wonder that each individual described has a unique characteristic that makes him or her an individual of merit in his or her own right. Adopt a serious tone when the book reflects the importance of not "laughing" at "me." (Note: There is a reference in the book to everyone being the same in the eyes of God. For use in public schools, you may want to skip reading this page. The story can still be useful with this omission.)

Discussion Questions

1. To which of the characters in the story could you most relate? Why?
2. Why is it important to understand our own personal reactions to others who look different, or have a disability, or are victims of teasing or harassment?
3. What considerations do we need to make as educators to ensure that we treat everyone fairly including students, staff, parents, and community members?

Facilitating the Discussion

1. Help participants identify with one or more of the characters and ask them to identify specific characteristics or similarities that help them relate. Encourage the discussion that we are most likely to respond positively to those who are "most like us" whether in looks, actions, economic status, and so on.
2. This discussion should center around the fact that we each have biases based on our own upbringing and personal experiences. Therefore, as educators we must consider how those biases affect our reactions. Do we truly accept individual differences?
3. Ask participants to brainstorm ways that they can (or could) be aware of their treatment of others based on perceived differences. For example, relate a story about a parent who expresses anger and ways that you've seen it handled. This might include using a calm voice to invite the person to take a moment to regroup and consider the issues they want to address, or giving the person some "space" so they can calm down. Share ideas that are generated and solicit interest in reading additional material on learning acceptance and making it work for the betterment of the students you serve, particularly in ensuring that no one in the school is harassed or bullied.

Other Metaphorical Uses or Parallels

This book can be used for various issues related to diversity (e.g., disabilities, race, culture, or ethnicity).

Illustrations

The illustrations are brightly colored and provide a beautiful backdrop for examining individual differences.

Recommended Background Reading

M. Froschl and N. Gropper, "Fostering Friendships, Curbing Bullying," *Educational Leadership* 56, no. 8: (1999), 72–75; E. Shellard, *Recognizing and Preventing Bullying* (Arlington, VA: Educational Research Service, 2002).

Insight into Action

If teachers are interested in a discussion group that is ongoing to address issues and concerns related to acceptance and to nontolerance of harassment and bullying, find someone to coordinate and lead that group (e.g., counselor). Support groups for students to develop and maintain a nonharassing environment may come from this group; someone may wish to sponsor it. Be sure to share ways that have been generated in discussion question 3 either via hard copy list, e-mail, or website.

HARASSMENT AND BULLYING: ACTIVITY 2

Purpose

The purpose of this activity is to examine what happens when students harass or bully another student.

Materials

- Book: C. Myers, *Wings* (New York: Scholastic, 2000). ISBN 0-590-03377-8

Abstract of the Children's Book

This powerful book shares the story of Ikarus Jackson, who looks different from other students in his school because he has wings. The power of another student who recognizes his beauty and supports him helps him to overcome the effects of being teased by other students.

Setting the Stage

1. Write one personal characteristic that you have that distinguishes you from others.
2. How would you feel (or did you feel) if someone teased you about that characteristic?

Notes on Reading the Book

The reading of this book should focus on the effects of the teasing that Ikarus receives from others and how he avoids the children who tease him.

Discussion Questions

1. How are the wings of Ikarus a metaphor for the unique characteristics that individual students bring to school?
2. What happens to a student's belief in his or her "wings" when other students tease about that unique characteristic?
3. What is the role of the educator in helping students to address harassment and bullying?

Facilitating the Discussion

1. Ikarus's wings represent the unique characteristics that each individual brings to school, whether it is a physical strength or challenge (e.g., cerebral palsy), an intellectual challenge or strength (e.g., being gifted). When peers tease or bully a student about his or her unique characteristic, it is difficult to see that characteristic as something unique to yourself. Students who are teased often withdraw and avoid others.
2. Ask educators to discuss ways that they can monitor student teasing, while helping to build an environment where students reject unacceptable behavior and monitor themselves. Discuss strategies (e.g.,

student court, recognition for good citizenship, kindness award) that are appropriate for your school community.

Other Metaphorical Uses or Parallels

This book suggests that life is different for each of us and Ikarus's wings are like the parts of us that are strong and want to soar, but for some reason we may be discouraged or not recognized.

Illustrations

The illustrations in this book invite close examination as they represent the various aspects of struggle that the individual goes through in trying to be himself or herself when others are cruel or unkind.

Recommended Background Reading

M. Goldberg, *Lessons from Exceptional School Leaders* (Alexandria, VA: Association for Supervision and Curriculum Development, 2001).

Insight into Action

Take the ideas generated in discussion question 3 and disseminate them to all faculty. Develop a plan for the school that will address the issues related to harassment and bullying. These might include a student led assembly, guest speakers, or creating a student court, and so on.

HARASSMENT AND BULLYING: ACTIVITY 3

Purpose

The purpose of this activity is to identify ways that teachers and administrators working with students and parents can address the hurtful and potentially dangerous effects of bullying.

Materials

- Book: B. C. McCain, *Nobody Knew What to Do: A Story about Bullying* (Morton Grove, IL: Albert Whitman, 2001). ISBN 0-8075-5711-0

Abstract of the Children's Book

This book tells the story of a boy's teasing and one child's efforts to figure out what to do. The child finally realizes that he can tell his teacher, and after he does, the teacher and the principal help the children to resolve the problem.

Setting the Stage

1. Think about a time when you heard one student teasing or harassing another and you turned a "deaf ear." Did you continue to think about whether you should have said something?
2. What do you think a teacher's role is in the use of hurtful language or teasing or harassment of one student to another?

Notes on Reading the Book

The book is an easy read that identifies teasing, the effects on the child being teased, and another child who knows it is wrong but is not sure how to help. The story should be read with a somber voice in the beginning and then a hopeful voice toward the end when the student asks his teacher for assistance and sees that help is forthcoming.

Discussion Questions

1. How typical is the child who hears the abuse but does not know what to do?
2. List three ways that you can let students know that you are available to listen and to provide guidance when others are causing pain or anguish to another.
3. List two to three ways that you think we can work together to create an environment that encourages cooperativeness and also

clearly lets students know that harassment is not acceptable and will not be tolerated.

Facilitating the Discussion

1. Elicit comments from teachers to bring them to the understanding that many students hear others being unkind but have concerns about telling for fear of retribution, ridicule, or being harassed themselves. However, you want them also to get to the discussion point that as the adults, and educated adults at that, we are responsible for teaching others that there are ways to resolve our differences.

2. Ask the participants to turn in their list of three ways that they provide guidance to students. Have a group read through and consolidate the ideas and share them with the whole faculty via e-mail or a hard copy for their individual files.

3. Put people in small groups. Ask them to brainstorm ways that they think the adults in the school can work together to encourage cooperativeness and to let students know that harassment is not acceptable and will not be tolerated. It is not sufficient to simply state that students who exhibit these behaviors will be given detention or be suspended. The overall climate of the school is a factor in diminishing the behavior and encouraging acceptance and cooperativeness among the students, faculty, and staff. Ask the group to determine if they want to write a plan that all will agree to follow in the development of student skills.

Other Metaphorical Uses or Parallels

This book can also be used to discuss issues such as classism, disabilities, or race, culture/ethnicity, which often factor into one student teasing another.

Illustrations

The illustrations are muted watercolors that provide a serious backdrop for the issue of bullying. Be sure to help participants focus on the change in the faces of the students when the adults intervene in a positive way.

Recommended Background Reading

J. Lipson, ed., *Hostile Hallways: Bullying, Teasing, and Sexual Harassment in School* (Washington, D.C.: AAUW Educational Foundation, 2001).

Insight into Action

The ideas generated in discussion questions 2 and/or 3 can be shared with the entire faculty and may lead to the development of a handbook or resource book for faculty and staff to promote acceptance and cooperativeness. This will be particularly helpful for new faculty who might not have been part of the development of the handbook or resource book.

VALUES EXPLORATION: ACTIVITY I

Purpose

The purpose of this activity is to explore the congruence between teachers' personal values and the values they judge as central to the community in which they teach.

Materials

- Book: J. J. Muth, *The Three Questions* (New York: Scholastic, 2002). ISBN 0-439-19996-4

Abstract of the Children's Book

A young boy turns to his animal friends to find answers to three questions about the right way to live. By the story's end he realizes, with the help of an old turtle, that he knew the answers, as they were evident in his behavior.

Setting the Stage

1. Very quickly, list your most enduring and deeply held school values. (No more than six, please.)
2. Number them, in order of priority, from the most to the least important.
3. Now, make a list, no more than six, please, of what you believe are the most enduring and deeply held values of the community in which you teach.
4. Number them, in order of priority, from the most to the least important.

Notes on Reading the Book

Sonya, the heron, represents a future perspective. Gogol, the monkey, represents a present orientation. Pushkin, the dog, represents a political orientation. Anyone, from a male with a booming voice to someone with a gentler tone, can read this book aloud effectively. The illustrations are gorgeous; the reader should take time for participants to view them.

Discussion Questions

1. How is your response to item 1 in Setting the Stage exemplified in your day-to-day activities?
2. What are the specific stressors, particularly those at school, that interfere with your ability to live according to your values?
3. What conflicts, if any, are evident in your responses to the first question and your response to the third?
4. Do your values emphasize a present or future orientation? Or, in other words, are your values something you work toward or something you already have?

Facilitating the Discussion

It is not uncommon for teachers, as busy professionals with families of their own, to have their priorities battered by day-to-day life. Ask teachers to examine the similarities and differences in their salaries and the community values they listed earlier. Probe for how teachers' expressed values affect school climate and culture and how value differences between teachers, administrators, and community members play out in conflict resolution, educational priorities, school policies, and curricular issues.

Other Metaphorical Uses or Parallels

1. This story can be used to address the value of being "other centered." Is it imperative to be "other centered" if you work in education?
2. Similarly, this work can be used to facilitate a conversation about one's willingness to give and receive help. Is it easier to help others than to ask for help when you need it?

Illustrations

Muth's watercolor illustrations are incredible. Take time to share them with the participants, particularly the last scene of the animals walking off with the boy.

Recommended Background Reading

W. Damon, "Teaching Values in School Promotes Understanding and Good Citizenship," *Brown University Child and Adolescent Behavior Letter* 8, no. 10 (1992): 3.

Insight into Action

Brainstorm some strategies that may help you refocus your energies on what is most important to you. How can the school community help teachers and students? Do your students, for example, provide a challenge to you living up to your espoused values?

VALUES EXPLORATION: ACTIVITY 2

Purpose

The purpose of this activity is to help participants consider how our different views as educators, parents, and community members need to be considered when we make decisions in the educational arena.

Materials

- Book: E. Young, *Seven Blind Mice* (New York: Philomel, 1992). ISBN 0-399-22261-8

Abstract of the Children's Book

This colorful book shares the story of seven blind mice who are trying to determine the "what" of something in their environment. Each goes off to try to assess the object and reports back with different views of what they found. The ending makes it clear that when each tries to understand the other's views, they can agree.

Setting the Stage

1. Think about a time when you were trying to describe something to another person and she or he did not understand what you were describing. How did you feel?
2. Are there times when you feel that you have to sacrifice your personal values in your work environment? If yes, write an example.

Notes on Reading the Book

Read the book with different voices for each of the colored mice (e.g., squeaky, loud, self-assured, haughty). When they search the elephant with the same understanding, use a voice that shows assurance, but not arrogance, thus indicating consensus.

Discussion Questions

1. How were the efforts of the mice to describe the object to each other similar to trying to figure out what students and their parents value?
2. Since grades are a social construct (that is, as people we give value to grades versus their being "necessary" for existence, like air), in what ways do your values as a teacher affect your view of the importance of grades?

3. What ways can we, as a group, work with parents to find the common ground for what we value related to completion of assignments, grades, and so on?

Facilitating the Discussion

1. Discuss with the participants that each of the mice had a particular point of view based on his or her personal experience. Each was confident that she or he was correct in describing the unknown object.
2. Discuss how grades are valued by teachers and many parents, but often have different values for teachers and students, students and parents, and so on. Discuss ways that faculty can ensure that there is an understanding of what grades are intended to convey. Also, discuss the role of teachers and students with regard to responsibility for grades.
3. Brainstorm ideas for informing parents and students of grading policies, the purpose of grades, and so on. Discuss differences among faculty about what grades are intended to convey. Try to identify ways that faculty can work together to improve the understanding of grades when teachers' views are different from parents; make sure that parents understand teachers' purposes of grades.

Other Metaphorical Uses or Parallels

This book can be used to discuss any issues that are in conflict in the school community. A dress code, for example, is often affected by the values of the family. Parents sometimes want schools to serve as the "clothes police" and others want their children to be able to wear whatever they want. A discussion on how different views affect this issue can occur with this book.

Illustrations

The illustrations are simple, but graphic of the magnitude of some issues (the elephant) versus the view of the one trying to describe the issue (the mouse).

Recommended Background Reading

D. R. Carlin, "Teaching Values in School," *Commonweal* 123, no. 3 (1996): 7.

Insight into Action

From discussion question 3, ask a committee to develop an action plan for issues that arise in the school community that result in a conflict of values. For example, the School Improvement Council may be the vehicle for concerns, or there may be a specific committee for community action that may exist or be formed. Be sure that there is a mechanism for informing all aspects of the community of the results of such meetings and/or actions.

VALUES EXPLORATION: ACTIVITY 3

Purpose

The purpose of this activity is to explore the core of family values and how they are altered based on circumstances. Given that this happens every day to the students in our schools, this activity will allow teachers and administrators to explore how the changes in family values can and do affect schooling.

Materials

- Book: P. Fleischman, *The Animal Hedge* (Cambridge, MA: Candlewick, 2003). ISBN 0-7636-1606-0

Abstract of the Children's Book

This book on the love of a father for his sons and for his land explores the devastation that besets them when a drought causes them to lose the farm. The result of this event finds the sons heading off to different kinds of employment in order to survive (e.g., going to sea). It is a poignant story of having to give up something you believe in so that you can survive.

Setting the Stage

1. Do you know a student or friend who has been affected by a job loss or loss of livelihood? How did this affect his or her values about the world of work?
2. How would you react or feel if you found out today that you, or someone you love, could no longer do the job/work she or he currently has? Would your values guide you? How?

Notes on Reading the Book

The book is a lovely story that requires a thorough read before trying to read it to a group for this activity. You may find that you want to paraphrase the book or "tell the story" with the illustrations, rather than read it verbatim, depending on the time available. Be sure the reader shows the strength of the father in teaching his boys early on and the struggle in letting them go, even when he knows he must. Think about giving voice to the acceptance the father could exhibit to the boys as "following their hearts" in the end.

Discussion Questions

1. How was the loss of the farm as unpredictable to the farmer as the loss of jobs can be to families in school? Can such losses affect the values the family shares about the importance of a child's schooling when the family is in crisis?
2. What ways can you share with each other to identify ways that people cope (like the animal hedge) when they feel they have no control of their life circumstances?
3. What is the role of teachers and others in the educational system in assisting students to stay focused on their own personal growth when the situations in their homes make it difficult for them to do so?

Facilitating the Discussion

1. Keep in mind the effects in our country of "downsizing" corporations, closing of factories, and general employment decline during

bad economic times. Help teachers consider the father's expectation that he would always own the farm and that his sons would be able to work and live there, too. Consider students who live in families with corporate midlevel management parents who may never even consider that their life circumstances can change quickly based on their parents' employment.

2. Ask teachers to brainstorm in small groups the coping strategies they have witnessed or can imagine when one's "world is turned upside down." Have them share those strategies and discuss how individuals drew on personal strength, support from others, belief in self and/or a higher being.

3. Often teachers do not realize the effects of such personal loss as a parent's employment (thus changing perhaps a lifetime of expectation) on a student's behavior, learning, or interactions. Explore the strategies that teachers can employ when they suspect a student may need help in identifying coping mechanisms.

Other Metaphorical Uses or Parallels

This book can also be used to discuss issues of hope and following one's dream. Focus on how the farmer found creative ways to cope with his loss of animals and his farm by developing a love of the animal hedge.

Illustrations

The illustrations are colorful and particularly beautiful in their representations as provided in the hedge. You might want to start out by showing the pages with the animal hedge and asking participants to decide what the story is going to be about.

Recommended Background Reading

A. Knafo, "Contexts, Relationship Quality, and Family Value Socialization: The Case of Parent–School Ideological Fit in Israel," *Personal Relationships* 10, no. 3 (2003): 371–89.

Insight into Action

Start a reading group that can contribute to the education of all in a number of ways. For instance, one group could be responsible for tracking the local and area news and economic situation and provide a "Working Notes" in the school's weekly (or daily) bulletin. Another group could be responsible for finding a few articles about schools that have dealt with other community or regional job loss situations and how they helped students cope. Last, but certainly not least, revisit the issue of conflict for students when the things their family believes or expects (in this case, work) are altered drastically.

SOCIETAL TRAUMA: ACTIVITY I

Purpose

The purpose of this activity is to help teachers brainstorm creative responses to societal traumas. This exercise emphasizes that we may not have control or influence over events in our lives, but we do have a say in how we respond to them.

Materials

- Book: J. J. Muth, *Stone Soup* (New York: Scholastic, 2003). ISBN 0-439-33909-X

Abstract of the Children's Book

Typically used as a story about sharing, *Stone Soup* tells of three monks who enter a village where the inhabitants are self-centered and suspicious of one another. The monks teach the villagers to share by gently urging individuals to contribute what they have to their "soup" made initially of stones and water. As the author notes, the story is told in Buddhist tradition, "where tricksters spread enlightenment rather than seeking gain for themselves."

Setting the Stage

Ask participants to write down their responses to the following questions:

1. Generally speaking, are you more comfortable giving or receiving assistance? Why?
2. Aside from academic or school-related issues involving your students, when was the last time you helped someone? How did you feel? How did they feel?
3. Have you ever been "helped" when you didn't want to be?

Notes on Reading the Book

Emphasize, via the storytelling, the reasons why the villagers are self-absorbed and suspicious of these monks.

Discussion Questions

1. Does "helping" demand reciprocity?
2. In building community is reciprocity important? Is there an honorable response to pity?
3. Can you build a community without sharing?
4. Can a focus on "the other" be spurred and nurtured within school? If so, how? If not, why not?
5. "They could not see from so far above that the village had been through many hard times." How might those in trouble hide their problems, especially in a school setting?
6. Did the villagers ask for help? Do you have a moral obligation to help, even if the person/people don't want to be helped, or somehow resist your efforts?
7. In what ways (historically) have U.S. communities helped after a tragedy?
8. How do the monks *specifically* entice villagers to contribute to the stone soup?

Facilitating the Discussion

At first reading, this story seems simplistic: everyone gives, everyone shares. Gently nudge respondents to go beyond their initial reading. See questions 4–8 on the previous page.

Other Metaphorical Uses or Parallels

Community building, teamwork, or multiculturalism are all appropriate applications of this story.

Illustrations

Jon Muth's watercolors are fabulous. In attending to the illustrations, pay attention to the notes at the book's end.

Recommended Background Reading

A. Etzioni, *The Spirit of Community: Rights, Responsibilities, and the Communitarian Agenda* (New York: Crown, 1993).

Insight into Action

Strategize ways to allow teachers, students, staff members, and families who are assisted in some way to give back to the school community. Strategize school problems that could be better addressed by group effort. What's holding you back?

SOCIETAL TRAUMA: ACTIVITY 2

Purpose

The purpose of this activity is to provoke a discussion of the extent and limits of children's resiliency through crises.

Materials

- Book: S. Steward, *The Gardener* (New York: Sunburst/Farrar Strauss Giroux, 1997). ISBN 0-3744251-8-3. A Caldecott Honor Book

Abstract of the Children's Book

In this story, told through letters and set during the Depression, a young girl is sent to live with her uncle in the city. Despite his dour mood, the girl attempts to make him smile by planting a garden on his rooftop. After a year of city life, Lydia Grace returns to her parents in the country.

Setting the Stage

1. No doubt, as a teacher, you've seen children whose lives were disrupted by divorce, family troubles, poverty, or death. What assumptions did you make when you heard of a student's problems from such trauma?
2. Were your assumptions accurate?
3. In your opinion, in what ways are children and youth particularly vulnerable to trauma? Make a list.

Notes on Reading the Book

The story, via pictures, begins in the front piece. Pay attention to the parents on the title page and to Uncle Jim wherever he appears. Since a girl narrates, a woman is probably the best choice to read this selection. At the start, affect should be sad, gaining optimism as the story progresses. Read slowly.

Discussion Questions

1. What elements of hardship are embedded in the story? How do you infer hardship from your students? Is it easy to read?
2. Lydia Grace survives for six months with unsmiling Uncle Jim before she discovers the roof. What does she do to survive until then?

3. Lydia Grace writes to her grandma, "I'm planning on a big smile from Uncle Jim in the near future." Does she get it? What does she get?
4. How does Lydia Grace survive?
5. In your opinion, is social trauma easier to overcome when it is on a large scale (the Depression) as opposed to more personal or familial tragedy?

Facilitating the Discussion

In what ways do we (inadvertently) truncate students' expressions of grief? What can be done to remedy that? What worked for Lydia Grace? Who (or what) helps Lydia Grace survive the year with Uncle Jim? In what ways are these significant? What can you take away from that, particularly since Lydia Grace continually turns to Uncle Jim for emotional reinforcement? What's the significance of "I've tried to remember everything you ever taught me."

Other Metaphorical Uses or Parallels

Family structures, creativity, and multiple intelligences are topics that can be addressed with this book.

Illustrations

Numerous subtexts live through the illustrations (Grandmother's face, terror in the station, the physical transformation of the bakery storefront, the role of the cat, starkness of interiors, desolation of the rooftop.)

Recommended Background Reading

D. McNamara, "Reaction to Traumatic Events Tied to Patient's Age (When Is It PTSD?)," *Pediatric News* 36, no. 9 (2002): 34–35.

Insight into Action

1. Brainstorm a list of activities and resources that may be made available to students and families. Do this before tragedy strikes.

Brainstorm various methods of disseminating these resources to those who may need them.

2. Look, in particular, for creative outlets, support systems, and community agencies that may be called on in a crisis. Make this list available to all teachers and other school staff.

SOCIETAL TRAUMA: ACTIVITY 3

Purpose

The purpose of this activity is to examine the ways in which a community comes together when a major catastrophe occurs.

Materials

- Book: J. H. Miller and T. Miller, *The Mighty Hugo Comes to Town* (New York: Jereleen H. Miller, 1994). ISBN 0-964300-0-9
- Paper and pens or pencils for each participant

Abstract of the Children's Book

This book tells the story of a mighty hurricane from the perspective of the storm itself. We rarely think about the elements of nature using the same characteristics that we consider when we try to understand the tragedies brought by humans. With the focus on the growth and development of the storm as it finds new and "interesting" things to destroy, the book shows the damage done when growth is not controlled (or controllable). The book also provides a good checklist for hurricane preparedness.

Setting the Stage

1. When you last heard that there had been devastation from a major storm or earthquake, did you think about how that element of nature developed? Why or why not?
2. In what ways are a developing storm and the academic growth of a student similar?

Notes on Reading the Book

The book provides the opportunity to "give life" to the storm by reading it from the early stages of its development as if it were a child looking for things to do (e.g., playing with the fishes) to a growing teenager when it goes in search of larger "things" with which to play. As the storm develops, it is important to give it a larger voice. The fear and angry voice of its ravages should become evident as the storm lashes the towns. As it fades away over the mountains, the reader should soften the voice as an indication of the quiet that follows the rage.

Discussion Questions

1. Why is the growth of the storm, from its origin as a playful swirling of water to the mighty Hugo, disconcerting in most people's minds?
2. What is one way that you can help students process the effects of a community tragedy?
3. Discuss ways that teachers can help students cope with the aftermath of a community tragedy (e.g., hurricane, tornado, earthquake).

Facilitating the Discussion

1. Discuss how we take things in nature for granted and even enjoy their beauty (e.g., the ocean) when it does not pose a threat. But when the elements come together to create a ravaging storm that disrupts life and destroys property, we lose sight of the beauty that we saw in the individual elements (e.g., the ocean, the wind).
2. Ask participants to list several ways, individually, that educators can help students cope with a community tragedy. Then pair/share and record the combined ideas.
3. Take the pair/share lists and discuss elements that would work in your community, whether specific to your school or to the community as a whole. For instance, if you are a high school faculty, you might be able to provide writing buddies for the elementary school via e-mail to explore ideas about helping your community heal from the tragedy.

Other Metaphorical Uses or Parallels

This book provides the opportunity to discuss conundrums that occur in many aspects of life, such as why a child can grow up to be abusive when she or he started out "just playing rough" with others.

Illustrations

The illustrations are extremely colorful and provide a great visual for the development of a playful wave into a mighty storm. Be sure that everyone gets the opportunity to see the graphics.

Recommended Background Reading

V. London, *Lucy and the Liberty Quilt* (Frisco, TX: Sparklesoup Studios, 2001).

Insight into Action

Review your emergency plan to ensure that it contains guidelines for dealing with the aftermath of a community tragedy. Often these plans prepare teachers and staff for the immediacy of the situation but do not provide steps for dealing with the needs of people afterward. Use the ideas developed in discussion question 3 as a basis for this component of your emergency plan.

SOCIETAL TRAUMA: ACTIVITY 4

Purpose

The purpose of this activity is to provide participants the opportunity to discuss the effects of societal trauma on everyone in the community and to examine ways that, in the aftermath, individuals can bring hope to others.

Materials

- Book: D. Shannon, *The Rain Came Down* (New York: Blue Sky, 2000). ISBN 0-439-05021-9

Abstract of the Children's Book

This book provides a wonderful example of how a traumatic event (in this case, rain) can have a strong effect on everyone from the animals to the people. The first part of the book describes the reactions of animals and humans to the rainstorm and the people's treatment of each other during the trauma, as each thinks only of himself. When the rain stops and the sun begins to shine, individuals begin to see ways that they could be helpful to each other and to feel the effects of a positive attitude.

Setting the Stage

1. Write three words that describe how you felt in a major traumatic event (e.g., 9/11, a tornado, flood, or the explosion of the *Challenger* space shuttle).
2. Can you think what your own personal immediate response is likely to be the next major societal trauma? Will it be self-preservation? Ways to help others? Ways to protect your property?

Notes on Reading the Book

The book is an easy read and the illustrations provide a great frame for each of the events during the trauma of the rain, as well as the hope that is evident after the storm. By reading it through once before the discussion, the reader will easily see how vocal expressions can strengthen the sharing of this story.

Discussion Questions

1. How does the forceful rain represent societal traumas that may have an effect on school?
2. After the rain, what characteristics of the individuals can be important for teachers when helping others to cope after a major school, community, or societal trauma?
3. What would benefit a faculty and school community in coping after a societal trauma, whether we are targets in the trauma or are affected by exposure to it (e.g., 9/11)?

Facilitating the Discussion

1. Elicit from the group their assumptions regarding traumas. The event is often unpredictable, is usually *not* what one would want to have happen, and can often be totally outside of our awareness or control.

2. Reactions and coping mechanisms that are evident in the characters include optimism (the baker, the woman in the taxi getting a new hairdo), returning to a routine (the pizza man, the truck driver delivering the tomatoes), supporting each other (the painter and the barber), ensuring a safe community (the police officer), going above and beyond normal duty (the ice cream man), and valuing what we do have (the family having a picnic).

3. Review (or develop) a school plan for action after a major school, community, or societal trauma. Does it include ways to ensure the responses identified in question two? Does it allow for the time that can be needed for all members of the community to heal and put the trauma in perspective?

Other Metaphorical Uses or Parallels

The rainstorm can also represent the speed with which things can happen, resulting in insecurity and distress. The changes in people after the storm can be helpful prompts to discuss ways to cope with the immediacy of some catastrophes.

Illustrations

The illustrations are bright and colorful and provide well-depicted expressions of the actions of both the people and the animals to the trauma of the rain. The pleasure and surprise when the "sunshine" appears is evident on the faces of the characters. Point out how various illustrations depict people who found ways to share their new found hope after the trauma.

Recommended Background Reading

National Center for Post Traumatic Stress Disorder (www.ncptsd.org).

Insight into Action

After reviewing (or developing) a school plan for the aftermath of trauma, provide a copy to all staff members and look for ways to ensure that it is reviewed regularly (e.g., have someone on staff be responsible for checking to see that everyone still feels reassured by the procedures). It is important to note that while most schools have emergency plans for traumatic events, which generally include counseling for staff and students afterward, there is rarely a chance for faculty to think through the human emotion that is inherent in dealing with traumas. Having done so, they are more likely to be able to rely on the plan to help themselves get through the aftermath.

THE WEIGHT OF POVERTY: ACTIVITY I

Purpose

The purpose of this activity is to address the need for teachers to recognize the unique abilities of each student to learn, create, and contribute even when faced with the challenges of poverty.

Materials

- Book: S. Taback, *Joseph Had a Little Overcoat* (New York: Penguin, 1998). ISBN 0-670-87855-3
- Chart paper
- Markers
- Paper and pens/pencils for each participant

Abstract of the Children's Book

Joseph has an overcoat that becomes old and tattered, but because he can not afford to waste anything, he becomes creative in his use of the material in the overcoat. Even when he has used the material from the overcoat for everything possible and loses the last item he made, he finds a way to make "something from nothing." This is a charming story of ingenuity and creativity in spite of poverty.

Setting the Stage

1. Identify three things you can do to "make something from nothing" in your classroom.
2. Write three words to describe a child who lives in poverty that you have taught.

Notes on Reading the Book

This is an easily readable book that tells the story of a man of poverty who is resourceful and creative in using what he has. Even when all that he has managed to create from a garment that gradually wears out, he finds a way to make "something from nothing." Read the book with a voice of awe at his ability to recycle what he has.

Discussion Questions

1. How did the book address the challenges of poverty?
2. How did the book address the effects of problem solving?
3. How did the book address the idea that you can "make something from nothing"?

Facilitating the Discussion

1. Help the participants to discuss the fact that when people are poor they often have to find ways to reuse what they have and to make do with very little.
2. Ask the participants to write down their own ideas from the previous discussion and then share them in a larger group, either in pairs or small groups. Record ideas on chart paper. Ask the participants to consider how willing they would be to reuse an item in as many ways as the story's protagonist.
3. Examine the ways that teachers, students, staff, and administrators could be more resourceful within the school by finding ways to make things from existing materials rather than expecting "store bought" or "new" products. Discuss how using materials in this way can validate those who "must" live this way, and develop creativity by thinking of ways to use what we have.

Other Metaphorical Uses or Parallels

This book is rich in its portrayal of Jewish symbols in the illustrations and can be used to discuss the differences in religious symbolism and how it affects schools. There is an activity in chapter 3 entitled "Religion" in this handbook.

Illustrations

The illustrations are beautiful and carefully crafted to provide a prompt for how the man will use what he has to create something else. The pictures also contain elements of Jewish life and culture. Pay special attention to the pages' cutouts that predict the newest transformation of Joseph's overcoat.

Recommended Background Reading

J. McKendrick, "Deep Impact (Effect of Poverty on Children)," *Community Care*, 2004, 24.

Insight into Action

Encourage teachers to find ways with their students to examine the ways that they can recycle and reuse materials, ideas, or projects to create something new and interesting. Submit an idea for a general list to be provided to all teachers or posted to a website. See if you can come up with some sort of award for interesting and creative ways to reuse things.

THE WEIGHT OF POVERTY: ACTIVITY 2

Purpose

The purpose of this activity is for participants to discuss the similarities among parents, regardless of how different they may be, rich or poor, in their dreams for their children.

Materials

- Book: M. D. Sander and T. Sillers, *I Hope You Dance!* (Nashville, TN: Rutledge Hill, 2003). ISBN 1-4016-0127-8
- Music: Lee Ann Womack, *I Hope You Dance* (MCA International, 2001).

Abstract of the Children's Book

This children's book expands on the popular song "I Hope You Dance" to provide a verbal and visual journey into the dreams of parents for their child. Often when dealing with children of poverty, teachers forget that those parents have dreams for their children, too. This book helps to spark the dream for all children that life is beautiful.

Setting the Stage

1. What is the thing or event in your life that caused you the most wonder?
2. In what ways do you explore the idea of dreams and aspirations with students?

Notes on Reading the Book

This book should be read by someone who can give voice to the excitement of a dream held by parents for their child. The words are catchy and funny. They should be read with the lilt provided in the language.

Discussion Questions

1. Do most parents have dreams for their children? Think of a child of poverty you have taught and the dreams that were expressed by his or her parents.
2. Consider the phrase, "I hope you dance." What are some of the educational things for which it could be a metaphor?
3. Identify interactions that you have with students that convey the message of hope expressed in the phrase, "I hope you dance."

Facilitating the Discussion

1. Either in a large group or small group forum, ask participants to discuss indicators of parents' dreams for their children. Have one or two share specific examples related to children of poverty. Emphasize the importance of not losing sight of the fact that dreams of self-improvement will contribute to students' achievement in academic activities or aspirations in spite of poverty.

2. "I hope you dance" can be a metaphor for many things. For example, it could mean: I hope you achieve good grades, or I hope you set high goals for yourself in seeking college admission, or I hope you perform to the best of your ability in an athletic competition. The point of this discussion is that there are many ways that students can "dance" in life and we need to help students find and celebrate them.

3. Either in the discussion session or by a date provided, have teachers write one or two ways that they believe they interact with students to convey that they too have a dream for each of their students.

Other Metaphorical Uses or Parallels

This book can also be used with the companion volume 2 on the topic of faculty work life to illustrate the importance of teachers having dreams for themselves.

Illustrations

The illustrations are colorful and cheery. Be sure to choose ones that you want the participants to see. The illustration concerning a parent's toupee is particularly useful to illustrate that all parents, no matter what their circumstances are, want good things for their children.

Recommended Background Reading

R. Kotulak, "Poverty Can Damage Children's Potential for Learning, Research Says," Knight Ridder/Tribune News Service, December 4, 2003, K4753.

Insight into Action

From the items submitted by teachers on ways that they interact with students to show that they have a dream for them, create a list that can be shared either on your web page or hard copies distributed to teachers. A particularly powerful web page could be made from these ideas with a heading like "Teachers at Our School Have the Following Dreams for Our Students" or a bulletin board in the school could be done with illustrated ideas for teachers' dreams for students.

THE WEIGHT OF POVERTY: ACTIVITY 3

Purpose

The purpose of this activity is to understand the myriad roots of poverty and explore its effects on children's educational success.

Materials

- Book: L. Riley, *Mouse Mess* (New York: Scholastic, 1997). ISBN 0-590-10048-3
- Paper and pencils for each small group of four to six participants

Abstract of the Children's Book

A small mouse makes himself at home in a kitchen. He creates havoc by spilling and dumping various foodstuffs and, in the end, denies any responsibility for the situation in which he finds himself. Instead of acting responsibly, he takes a bath and goes back to bed.

Setting the Stage

1. Why are people in your community economically poor? Brainstorm a list.
2. Get into small groups of four to six. Combine or collate your lists.
3. Analyze your combined lists according to attribution of cause: (1) personal choices and values, (2) community limitations (e.g., few

jobs), (3) economic structure and norms (e.g., low wages for service jobs), (4) historical or familial norms (e.g., children learn what they live), or (5) other.

4. Which category was most prominent among your lists? Why?

Notes on Reading the Book

The text is short and rhyming. The reader should read the text with a playful cadence, being sure to share the rich illustrations with participants.

Discussion Questions

1. How do you suspect the mouse got into the house? Is the mouse a visitor or a permanent resident?
2. What assumptions do we make about the figures on the stairs?
3. Whose food is it? Does the mouse have a right to eat?
4. How do you view the mouse? How would you view the offspring of the mouse?
5. Do you suspect the people in the background know that a mouse has taken up residence in their home? Do they bear any responsibility for the "mouse mess"?

Facilitating the Discussion

Emotions may run hot with this activity. The goal is to allow people to express their frustrations regarding the persistence of poverty in American communities. Generally, understandings about the causes of poverty tend to cluster in two separate camps, often aligned with two political perspectives. The first, a conservative perspective, assumes that the root causes of poverty stem from poor personal choices. The second, a liberal perspective, assumes that the root causes stem from inequitable social structures, as well as inequities in the political and economic structure of the American economy and political system. In order to bring order to the chaos, the facilitator should look for commonalities in the meaning of the responses to the problem of poverty. For example, is there widespread consensus that children are not to blame for the situations into which they are born? If we expect children to learn from adults, can they be held accountable for the lessons they internalize from their parents or other adult role models? Despite the focus on affect, the larger aim, however, is to move beyond emotion to a broader understanding of poverty's root causes.

In discussion question 1, it is important to remember that the mouse—poverty—has always been there. In discussion question 4, have the participants think about entitlements. Does corporate America enjoy entitlements?

Other Metaphorical Uses or Parallels

The mouse can symbolize how play to one person may be interpreted or experienced as work by another. The story may also be used to probe discussions of the assumptions and avoidance of responsibility, particularly professional responsibility.

Illustrations

Through colorful cutouts, the author captures the colors and textures of popular foodstuffs, as well as the chaotic mess created by the mouse. Be sure to share the illustrations generously, as they are so rich. In addition, without much accompanying text, the illustrations denote a family of four retreating, and reentering, by a staircase in the background.

Recommended Background Reading

B. Ehrenreich, *Nickled and Dimed: On (Not) Getting By in America* (New York: Holt, 2002). For an excellent discussion of the effects of poverty and efforts to close the achievement gap, particularly efforts in minority and low income schools, see K. Haycock (2001), "Closing the Achievement Gap," *Educational Leadership* 58, no. 6: 6–11.

Insight into Action

Follow up with session participants regarding what conversations, if any, they had about this topic with peers. What were the overarching concerns and perspectives? Is any common understanding emerging about the root causes of poverty?

CLASSISM: ACTIVITY I

Purpose

The purpose of this activity is to discuss the relationship of individual differences and perceived social standing.

Materials

- Book: M. Wynn, *The Eagles Who Thought They Were Chickens* (Marietta, GA: Rising Sun, 1993). ISBN 1-880463-12-1
- Paper and pencil for each participant
- Chart paper (tape if needed to post)
- Markers

Abstract of the Children's Book

To understand the power of what each of us brings to an environment and the importance of individual differences and celebration of cultures, this book provides a beautiful illustration of how eagles (considered so beautiful in our society) are scorned and ridiculed when placed in a new environment.

Setting the Stage

1. Write the names of three students who you believe "soar" above all the rest.
2. Write the names of three students whose behaviors remind you of crows.
3. Write the names of three students you've taught who seem to have always been "scratching around" for their place in the classroom, bringing attention to themselves through seemingly senseless behaviors.

Notes on Reading the Book

After reading the book through once, you will be able to see the importance of the inflection you will need to provide in the mocking words of the chickens and the proud voice of the eagles early on and then the soft, shy voice of the eagle when it is clear that acceptance is not going to happen.

Discussion Questions

1. Why do we hold the eagle in such high esteem? Do all nations revere the eagle the way Americans do?
2. Who are the eagles in school? Who are the crows? Who are the chickens? Can we make the chickens into eagles?
3. What actions do we take (or behaviors do we encourage) that clearly result in some students being viewed as eagles and others as crows?

Facilitating the Discussion

1. This discussion should be pretty straightforward, but issues of grace of flight, majestic size, "identity as our national bird" should come from it. No, not all nations revere the eagle.
2. Help teachers think about the characteristics that caused them to identify individuals or groups as one "bird" or another. Who helps maintain those stereotypes? Why? Discuss how the adults in the environment encourage, or discourage, classifying individuals. Discuss how teachers can facilitate students' practice of acceptance of individuals by the actions they exhibit.
3. Have individuals make a list first and then pair/share and then put on chart paper information that can then be discussed in the group and commonalities identified and considered.

Other Metaphorical Uses or Parallels

The book can be used to discuss issues of diversity related to race, culture, or ethnicity to emphasize that our uniqueness makes us different not inferior.

Illustrations

The only illustration in this book is its cover of a majestic eagle.

Recommended Background Reading

J. Banks, "The Historical Reconstruction of Knowledge about Race: Implications for Transformative Teaching," *Educational Researcher* 24, no. 2 (1995): 15–25.

Insight into Action

Take the ideas generated in discussion question 3 and either put on a discussion board or type up and distribute to teachers. Think of a professional development activity that faculty could conduct to problem solve how to honor each student's social class and discuss ways that individuals can be successful in crossing over socioeconomic lines.

CLASSISM: ACTIVITY 2

Purpose

The purpose of this activity is to have teachers and administrators consider, through self-reflection, how they developed their belief systems of "class" and how they make decisions on a daily basis that may inadvertently infer, or imply, that one social class has more personal value than another.

Materials

- Book: Y. M. Barnwell, *No Mirrors in My Nana's House* (Orlando, FL: Harcourt Brace, 1998). ISBN 0-15-201825-5
- Pictures of three to six children representative of different socioeconomic levels in a PowerPoint or on an overhead transparency (e.g., one child whose parents are wealthy, one whose parents are middle class, and one whose parents are poor). Ideally all pictures would be on one page (or might be posted in the room). These can be easily found on the Internet or in magazines such as *National Geographic*.

Abstract of the Children's Book

The beauty of the language in this book is based on the self-identity a little girl develops based solely on the "reflections" of her grandmother. The story provides a powerful message about the influence that adults can have on children and how they develop perceptions of self and others.

Setting the Stage

1. Think about the statements "I do not see color" or "I am 'color blind' because race is not important to me." Have you thought this or known others who have stated this?
2. Think about the following questions: Which child do you believe will come to school "ready to learn?" Which child will have the greatest likelihood for economic success? Which child will provide you the greatest challenges in teaching? Post each of the pictures with a number so teachers can see them as they consider the questions.

Notes on Reading the Book

This book was published following the success of the song by the same name. A very powerful way of presenting the book is to use the music with the illustrations, thus not having to give "voice" to the story other than the music.

Discussion Questions

1. How does the line that "I didn't know that my clothes didn't fit?" speak to the challenges that students of poverty face? Are clothes related to "class" for students?
2. What beliefs do you have that are "class" related and that you have worked to overcome, or want to overcome?
3. What issues in school are class related? Can (or should) these issues be addressed so that each student can feel that she or he is in a safe and accepting learning environment?

Facilitating the Discussion

1. Students of poverty do not expect to be able to choose the clothes they wear because they are almost always "hand-me-downs" or gifts from others (e.g., charitable groups). Discuss the challenges in a learning environment when some students have clothes that are highly promoted on television or in the ads and others do not.

2. Most teachers certainly can relate to "lifestyles of the rich and famous" as a "nonreality" for themselves. Discuss how it is easier as an adult to be satisfied, content, and even like your current economic level. But, for some, not ever thinking they have the "possibility to be rich" may influence how they treat children of wealthy parents.

3. Brainstorm a discussion on situations in school that teachers relate to class differences (e.g., the type of clothing some students wear that has the latest designer label). How can teachers, depending on the age of the students, have an impact on minimizing the "value" placed on those situations by others when we live in a materialistic society?

Other Metaphorical Uses or Parallels

Help teachers consider the effect of phrases that are prevalent in our society that reflect biases in different ways, for example, viewing others through "rose-colored glasses," "seeing yourself in others," or "he's a bad reflection on his parents."

Illustrations

The illustrations use strong, vibrant colors to depict the people in the story, but there are no faces. The last picture where the child is told "look into my eyes" is more poignant for the lack of facial features.

Recommended Background Reading

E. Lee, D. Menkart, and M. Ozazawa-Rey, *Beyond Heroes and Holidays: A Practical K–12 Antiracist, Multicultural Education, and Professional*

Development (Washington, D.C.: Network of Educators on the Americas, 1998).

Insight into Action

From the brainstorm session, create a discussion group and perhaps a "book study" to examine ways in which you can address issues of class in your school and in our society in general. If needed, create activities that can be conducted to ensure that students are aware of the impact of class (e.g., in a social studies unit) and limitations that actions of class place on all individuals in a society.

CLASSISM: ACTIVITY 3

Purpose

The purpose of this activity is to examine participant's assumptions regarding the last taboo, classism, particularly the myths and enduring realities of power and privilege.

Materials

- Book: J. Feiffer, *The House across the Street* (New York: Michael di Capua/Hyperion Books for Children, 2002). ISBN 0-7868-0910-8
- Two sheets of typing paper per participant
- Tape
- 3x5 cards
- Scissors
- 5x8 cards
- Colored markers
- Wooden craft sticks
- Glue
- Pencils

Abstract of the Children's Book

A young boy imagines the endless possibilities and fantastic options for, the boy who lives in the "big high house" across the street. The protagonist describes the family life of his neighbor, although his only meeting with the boy is in his imagination.

Setting the Stage

1. Divide the participants into four groups—A, B, C, and D. Divide each alphabetical group into small teams of three to five members.
2. Give to each small team of D group:
   a. Two sheets of typing paper
   b. A role of tape
   c. Ten 3×5 cards
   d. A pair of scissors
   e. Ten 5×8 cards
   f. Colored markers
   g. Twenty wooden craft sticks
   h. Glue
   i. Pencils
3. Give to each small team of C group items a–f.
4. Give each small team of B group items a–d.
5. Give each small team of A group items a and b only.
6. Emphasize the rules: You may not change groups. You may not speak to members outside your own category. You may use only the materials given to your team.
7. Your charge: *To construct, as a small group, the best model of a house that you can with the supplies you've been given. You have ten minutes.*

Notes on Reading the Book

Read slowly, with a strong voice that becomes more excited as the story progresses.

Discussion Questions

1. Did you or your team members look over or notice what supplies the other categories' team had? If so, how did you feel?
2. Were you frustrated by the supplies you were given or did you just push ahead?

3. Was the presence or lack of supplies a larger concern to some group's members than others? Were you temped to "cheat"?
4. Did some in your group try to "discount" the activity?
5. After the houses have been built, compare them. Did available supplies affect the sophistication or quality of the model? Are you surprised about how good (or how poor) some of the models are? Is the adequacy of the models directly reflective of the amount and variety of resources the group had? Why or why not? In what ways, if at all, do social clues of students shape your answers?

Facilitating the Discussion

This exercise is not about building a house. Rather, the intent is to provoke reactions from participants as they are asked to construct something with various amount and types of resources. What is important, as you let the participants view the various models, in the level of *affect* displayed by participants? Encourage expressions of equity, and probe for rationale behind the arguments. That is the message and power of this exercise.

Other Metaphorical Uses or Parallels

This book can be used to discuss team building with an emphasis on how difficult it can be when we have different values.

Illustrations

Focus on the first and last pages of the illustrations.

Recommended Background Reading

L. E. Beyer, ed., *Creating Democratic Classrooms: The Struggle to Integrate Theory and Practice* (New York: Teachers College Press, 1996); N. Schniedewinde and E. Davidson, *Open Minds to Equality: A Sourcebook of Learning Activities to Affirm Diversity and Promote Equality*, 2nd ed. (Boston: Allyn & Bacon, 1998).

Insight into Action

Teachers need to reflect on the assumptions that are made regarding social class diversity in their classrooms. Is one's social class important among students? Among teachers? How is membership in a social group expressed at your school? Does social class dictate small group membership? Why or why not?

CLASSISM: ACTIVITY 4

Purpose

The purpose of this activity is to aid teachers' understanding of the power and influence of students' cultural backgrounds, specifically their class background, in order to foster a dialog about class subcultures in a multicultural society.

Materials

* Book: A. H. Scott, *On Mother's Lap* (New York: Clarion, 1992). ISBN 0-395-58920-7

Abstract of the Children's Book

In simple, direct language, this book tells the story of a little boy who finds great comfort in sitting in his mother's lap. He particularly likes holding, while cuddled in his mother's lap, those things that are most precious to him. When his mother suggests making room for baby sister, the boy balks and asserts that there is no more room. His mother gently reminds him that there is always room in her lap for all of her children. (Note: The story is *not* the focus of this exercise, but rather the illustrations, which were inspired by the illustrator's visit to an Eskimo village.)

Setting the Stage

1. Tell session participants simply, "Write a paragraph about clotheslines."

2. In groups of three or four, analyze, from a cultural perspective, what these paragraphs say. For example, do these paragraphs talk about who uses clotheslines? Are judgments or perspectives inherent in what is written? Where are clotheslines usually seen? How many paragraphs reflect personal experience versus observations or assumptions? What assumptions, either positive or negative, are evident in these paragraphs?

Notes on Reading the Book

Because the focus of this activity is the illustrations rather than the story, special emphasis should be placed on giving participants ample opportunity to view the illustrations. The story should be read slowly and methodically, emphasizing the back-and-forth rhythm of the rocking chair.

Discussion Questions

1. As the story began and you saw the cover and the first illustrations, what ideas did you have regarding the likely story line? Was your impression shaped by what you saw (illustrations) or what you heard (the title)?
2. What values or practices are exemplified in this book? Do those values transcend class or cultural boundaries?
3. Is there any significance to the illustrations that tell us that the bedroom is the laundry room and the living room? Does it matter to the story line?

Facilitating the Discussion

Students' cultural backgrounds, and their membership in a subculture, color virtually every aspect of their school experience. School staff members are not always aware of, or sensitive to, the power that these memberships have for children. The power of classism, and staff members' inability to understand that power, can be a source of profound alienation for students.

1. Are value judgments associated with something so simple as how people do their laundry?

2. Were some of those assumptions evident in the paragraphs written by participants about clotheslines?
3. Does anyone, in their paragraph, write about having a clothesline as a child, or about using one now? Was (or is) the use of a clothesline out of necessity, or was (is) it a choice?
4. Why do some residential areas have protective covenants that restrict or forbid outdoor clotheslines?
5. What values or practices are exemplified in this book? Do those values transcend cultural or class boundaries?

Other Metaphorical Uses or Parallels

This story is a powerful exemplar of the universality of motherhood and the boundlessness of heart. Despite the child's concern about the limits of the size of a parental lap, the message of acceptance and unconditional love transcend physical limitations. This message is also particularly appropriate to underscore a major issue in sibling relationships: the sharing of parental attention and love. Finally, this story can also be used with students to help them understand that they are each special and unique; mother's lap can be a metaphor for their place in the world. Their talents and the totality of their being are important and vital. Despite concerns to the contrary, each child should be welcomed into the lap of humanity.

Illustrations

The style of the drawings, a combination of chalk with fine line drawings, gives the illustrations a special delicacy and power. Focus particular attention on the title page (which provides the largest perspective on the home's interior), pages 4–5, 16–17, (which include the interior clothesline), as well as pages 14–19 and 20. The depiction of naked bedsprings and the scarcity of material possessions contrast markedly to the richness of the familial relationships that is the bedrock of this story.

Recommended Background Reading

Ruby Payne's work on the contrasting primary values of different social classes is a must read for teachers and anyone working in schools.

Her work clearly delineates the contrasting values and assumptions that undergird class structure in American society. R. Payne, *Framework for Working with Students and Adults from Poverty* (Highlands, TX: aha! Process, 1995).

Insight into Action

The use of a clothesline is embraced to illustrate the profound assumptions that underlie social norms. By using the metaphor of the clothesline, teachers are encouraged to examine how their assumptions about how membership in a particular social class influences virtually every interpretation made about needs, wants, and what's important in life.

Working as a committee of the whole, ask teachers to identify aspects of the school's physical environment, as well as the school's social environment, that are deliberately (or unconsciously) created by school leaders. What do visitors first see when they walk into the school? Does that image convey a message about what social values are most important? How are the majority group's cultural values made evident in the school? (For example, what background music is played in the lobby, if any? What artwork, if any, is displayed? If commercial images are posted anywhere, what values, priorities, or aesthetics are evident? What types of food are commonly served in the cafeteria? Does the menu reflect food choices common in multicultural communities? Are books available to students that portray and value the home environments from which they come, or do most all stories center on middle- or upper-middle-class themes and lifestyles?

Finally, what does it mean that so many suburban subdivisions forbid, in their restrictive covenants, the use of clotheslines?

CLASSISM: ACTIVITY 5

Purpose

The purpose of this activity is to consider the historical effects of class as evidenced by the role that Chinese workers were assigned in building the railroads of this country. The activity will also provide an opportunity to identify the class lines that currently exist in the community in which the school operates.

Materials

- Book: Yin, *Coolies* (New York: Philomel, 2001). ISBN 0-399-23227-3

Abstract of the Children's Book

This beautifully written book shares the story of Chinese workers who came to the United States in search of an economic opportunity that was not available to them in China in the 1800s. They brought their culture and traditions with them and tried to live them in spite of the fact that their work environment provided a Eurocentric expectation for behavior.

Setting the Stage

1. If you have traveled outside of the United States, what experience has had the most impact on you? If you have not traveled outside the United States, what aspect of a culture that is foreign to you do you find most intriguing?
2. Are there vestiges of the melding of cultures in the United States? Name one or two things that support this view.

Notes on Reading the Book

The book is long and may take as long as twenty minutes to read. If the time is available, that is the best way to share the book. If time is short, read the book several times yourself and then "tell the story." You might choose several passages that are particularly illustrative of the language of the story. For example, the passage that describes the celebration of the meeting of the railroads and how everyone was invited except the Chinese, "not the coolies."

Discussion Questions

1. In the community, what are the current groups that would be the "coolies" of our time (i.e., those on whom we depend for work but otherwise ignore)?
2. Are there individuals who break the stereotype of a particular cultural group and have a positive impact on the community?
3. In what ways do we diminish another's culture within the context of the educational program/curriculum?

Facilitating the Discussion

1. Help the group identify individuals or work groups that are basically ignored by the larger community. A typical example is those who collect our trash or garbage. They provide a necessary function, but assumptions are often made that these individuals can't do anything else and therefore are not worthy of attention.
2. Try to identify individuals who have beaten the odds of the cultural community and been successful: for example, the first Asian mayor, or the first African American principal or superintendent.
3. Ask teachers within grade levels or departments to do a serious search of the text materials and supplemental materials they use to see if there is equal representation of ethnic groups, gender, and so on, within the content of the books. Have them share ways that they can supplement materials that are required to ensure that all groups are represented and valued.

Other Metaphorical Uses or Parallels

This book can also be used in the section on diversity to examine the contributions of Chinese immigrants to this country.

Illustrations

The illustrations are richly detailed and colorful representations of the travails of working on the railroad and also represent the effort to maintain and encourage the cultures brought into this nation.

Recommended Background Reading

C. M. Shields, "Learning from Difference: Considerations for Schools as Communities," *Curriculum Inquiry* 30, no. 3 (2000): 275–95.

Insight into Action

From discussion question 3, ask teachers to share their findings on text materials and ways that they can provide additional materials that honor all aspects of the community and contributions of different groups to our nation.

DEATH, DIVORCE, AND LOSS: ACTIVITY I

Purpose

The purpose of this activity is to provide a framework for discussing the inevitability of death. Suggestions are provided to encourage an honest discussion about death with students, particularly within the constraints inherent in a public school environment.

Materials

- Book: S. Varley, *Badger's Parting Gifts* (New York: Mulberry, 1984). ISBN 0-688-11518-7

Abstract of the Children's Book

Badger is much loved by all of the animals in the forest, but he is getting old. He acknowledges and accepts his impending death, and when it comes, he leaves his old body behind. His death, while accepted by him, is devastating to all of his friends. As they all work through their grief, they come to understand the value of Badger's friendship, the unique gifts he left each of them, and the importance of memory in coping with profound loss.

Setting the Stage

Inform participants that they will not need to share these results of this activity unless they wish to.

1. Think of something that you've lost in the past. It could be a person, a physical object of great value, or and intangible entity that you held dear.
2. Describe your immediate reaction when you were confronted with that loss. How did you feel?
3. To what extent, if at all, did you share your feelings and reactions with others? If you kept your feelings to yourself, why?
4. Did you share your feelings with others? If so, what were the reactions of the people closest to you, particularly those people who surrounded you during that period? Did they acknowledge your feelings and reactions, or ignore or dismiss them?

Notes on Reading the Book

The reader selected for this text should be sensitive to the myriad feelings that can accompany discussions of death and dying. The reader should be able to convey the death of Badger in a solemn tone, and gradually change one's affect as his friends recall their happy memories of Badger.

Discussion Questions

1. How has your earliest experience(s) of loss, death, or divorce shaped how you deal with loss as an adult? Have your experiences early in your life prepared you well to cope with loss? Why or why not?
2. To what extent, if at all, is our acceptance of death shaped by our ideas of what happens afterward? How are these ideas shared within the community in which you live?
3. What are some of the interpretations in the community or school about what happens when you die? How are those interpretations manifested within the school environment?

4. If loss, particularly the death of a student, has been a schoolwide concern in the past, how was it presented and handled? What worked and what didn't?
5. How can discussions of loss, particularly death, be handled by faculty and staff members if their own interpretations are religious in nature?

Facilitating the Discussion

Discussion around this text is likely to take two divergent, yet somewhat related, avenues, since this is one of the few children's books in which the death of a central character not only occurs but is also interpreted and described in great detail. Teachers may object to the "secular" description and its lack of reference to a deity. However, this is part of the value of this book, as it does not preclude an interpretation of such overtones for those who see death in religious terms. The second avenue concerns the grief process of those left behind. Through the discussion, teachers should be encouraged to acknowledge the wide variety of responses to death and the grieving process, as well as the importance of helping students acquire an emotionally healthy perspective on these processes. It is important that the facilitator help participants process their sometimes conflicting feelings about death and dying, as it is only when school personnel can acknowledge the complexity of their own feelings that they are likely to feel confident in their ability to be truly helpful to students who are experiencing loss and grief. The text itself can serve as a model for students in how to focus on the gifts left behind after a loss—even one so seemingly transitory, such as changing teachers or schools—and the power of memories to place the loss in a larger context.

Other Metaphorical Uses or Parallels

Any kind of change is a loss of sorts, as any new beginning is the end of something else. This book could be used to probe a discussion of resistance to change, as well as discussions of the resiliency of friendship, the importance of community, and the continuity of life.

Illustrations

The pictures prior to and during Badger's death are particularly rich and meaningful. The smaller pictures that face the full page illustrations have their own power and are worth noting.

Recommended Background Reading

Elisabeth Kubler-Ross, *On Death and Dying* (New York: Scribner, 1997); M. Colgrove, H. H. Bloomfield, and P. McWilliams, *How to Survive the Loss of a Love* (New York: Prelude, 1995).

Insight into Action

Create a forum in which teachers can share with others their handling, both positive and negative, of helping students cope with loss. This forum might be a schoolwide website, a log available to teachers in a staff room, or a topic of discussion in faculty meetings. Particular emphasis might need to be placed on scripting public school teachers with strong religious views to respond honestly, yet respectfully, to students about death, all the while respecting the separation of church and state. Clearly stated policies regarding proselytizing should be readily available and understood by all, and questions and concerns directed to appropriate district personnel.

DEATH, DIVORCE, AND LOSS: ACTIVITY 2

Purpose

The purpose of this activity is to explore the difficulty of change, particularly from a child's point of view.

Materials

- Book: J. Viorst, *Alexander, Who's Not (Do You Hear Me? I Mean It!) Going to Move* (New York: Scholastic, 1995). ISBN 0-590-89982-1

Abstract of the Children's Book

Alexander laments the fact that his family is moving 1,000 miles away due to his dad's new job. Although other family members have accepted the reality of the change, Alexander explores ways to stay behind. Eventually, with the help of his family, he agrees to move just one more time.

Setting the Stage

1. Take a few minutes to remember when you were a child.
2. Think of one element of your home life that you didn't really like.
3. How did you cope? Was that element something with which you had to struggle?
4. What effect did that reality have on your growing-up years?
5. How does that experience shape how you understand and respond to children who may be going through the same thing?

Notes on Reading the Book

As a read-aloud book, this is a long text. The best reader for this book is an extroverted soul who isn't too shy to read some of this text as a shout: "I'm *not* going to move." Take time to focus on Alexander's facial features.

Discussion Questions

1. Were you able, in any way, to change the realities that shaped your childhood?
2. Given the school population that you serve, what are some of the changes that students experience? How do they act on that experience?
3. How do you know how they feel? How do you respond? Are those responses helpful or healthy?

Facilitating the Discussion

1. Although the book addresses a family's move, the intent of the discussion is to move beyond family relocation to examine the effects

that other changes, particularly those that are unwanted, have on students (and, by extension, teachers).

2. As powerless as adults feel regarding events over which they have no control (e.g., job loss, contested divorce), adults are certainly more powerful to exert choice than are children who, by definition, are dependent on parents.

3. In this book, the protagonist's parents are married. How does a move affiliated with a divorce affect children? Is there anything teachers and other school staff can do to mitigate the affects of divorce on children? Are services available on the school site to help students cope with change, whether it is due to relocations, divorce, or other trauma?

Other Metaphorical Uses or Parallels

This text addresses a child's reluctance to accept a family move. It can also be used to discuss family dynamics and management of emotions.

Illustrations

Focus attention on those illustrations in which Alexander demonstrates particularly strong affect.

Recommended Background Reading

S. Johnson, *Who Moved My Cheese?* (New York: Putnam, 2002).

Insight into Action

Are groups conducted at the school site for children who are experiencing transitions? If not, why not? Many students benefit greatly from knowing that others are going through the same experience, be it divorce, familial stress, or a family member's deployment due to military obligations. Make sure that lists of social services that provide counseling to children and families are available to all school staff, not simply the school counselor or social worker.

DEATH, DIVORCE, AND LOSS: ACTIVITY 3

Purpose

The purpose of this activity is to help teachers and staff explore issues that arise when students and peers are dealing with loss, whether through death, divorce, relocation, or family upheaval.

Materials

- Book: P. Schwiebert and C. DeKlyen, *Tear Soup: A Recipe for Healing after Loss* (Portland: Grief Watch, 1999). ISBN 0-9615197-6-2

Abstract of the Children's Book

This book provides a "recipe" for the stages of grief whether the loss is death, divorce, ending of a relationship, or relocation. Grandy, the main character in the book, is a gentle soul who creates a framework for the use of tears and other emotions (e.g., wanting to be alone) when dealing with loss.

Setting the Stage

1. Write three words that express an emotion you remember feeling when you think of a personal loss you've experienced, whether it was through divorce, moving away or, death.
2. Is there a time frame that is "right" for dealing with loss?
3. If there is one thing you would tell others about a loss experience that could help them learn from your experience, what would it be?

Notes on Reading the Book

The reader should be able to give "voice" to the character of Grandy. (Note: The book is available on video if you prefer to present it that way. The ISBN is provided under the illustration description below.) While experiencing the pain of loss, the steps that Grandy provides in her "recipe" for tear soup also signal hope, so it is important not to have the reader limit the voice of Grandy to despair.

Discussion Questions

1. How do the steps in Grandy's recipe help us as educators think about the life events that students (or colleagues) experience?
2. Are there events in school, day to day, that require attention related to loss? What behaviors on the part of students (or colleagues) might signal that loss is affecting his or her performance or attitude?
3. Under what circumstances would you, as a classroom teacher, deal with issues of loss?
4. Do we have a support system for each other in dealing with issues related to loss?

Facilitating the Discussion

1. The steps in Grandy's recipe provide a framework for looking at the grief process and understanding that each individual progresses through them differently.
2. Help teachers brainstorm events in school, day to day, that require attention related to loss, such as the behaviors of another person that may signal loss (apathy, anger, lashing out, skipping school, etc.) This can be accomplished by having them pair and share and then share with the larger group.
3. The discussion of this question should lead to recognizing when teachers should engage a student about his or her loss (e.g., "Samantha, it appears to me that you are a little sad today. Is there some way I can help?"), to the major issues that affect everyone in a school when a student, staff member, or faculty is critically ill or dies. By having this discussion *before* something happens in a school family, it will be easier for staff to consider their actions when/if something happens.
4. This question provides the framework for discussing the system that is in place (e.g., school counselors) to explore what might be a good system for your environment to support each other in deal-

ing with issues related to loss (e.g., setting up a system that is different if it is a staff member versus a student, or if the loss involves multiple people within the schooling environment).

Other Metaphorical Uses or Parallels

The book is also extremely useful for dealing with the whole issue of understanding that changes in our lives can be difficult and require time to process. If your building is being renovated, and teachers have to give up the space to which they are accustomed, they may be excited initially about having a new building. Eventually, however, they may experience a sense of loss for what was familiar in the old space, which can be exacerbated by the disruptions of the renovation process.

Illustrations

The illustrations in the book are comforting as they depict a "lived-in" home with various elements that are traditional in the American home, but showing evidence of the elements of the grief process. For example, the canister set in the kitchen has labels that read: "not fair," "bad news," "big disappointment," "serious heartache," "profound loss," "major tragedy," "more than I can bear." These illustrations provide the visual to help teachers and staff focus on the many issues that surround loss and are powerful reminders of the humanity affected by loss. The book is also available on video from the publisher (ISBN 0-9724241-0-5).

Recommended Background Reading

The website www.griefwatch.com provides a wealth of information on issues related to death and dying. The website at www.nassp.org has information to help faculty and staff address issues of death and trauma that can occur in schools.

Insight into Action

Two of the discussion questions require particular attention in bringing action from this discussion. First, provide all teachers with a list of behaviors that signal possible loss. This can be collected from the discussion question and then disseminated to all teachers. Second, the elements of a support system that were generated in the discussion should be taken by a smaller group and fleshed out into a plan that can be brought back to the group for further refinement and adoption.

DEATH, DIVORCE, AND LOSS: ACTIVITY 4

Purpose

The purpose of this activity is to help participants explore the reactions of students and peers when death occurs for someone in the school community. Regardless of personal religious beliefs, it is possible to have hope that comes of love and understanding of the human condition.

Materials

- Book: W. Hanson, *The Next Place* (Minneapolis: Waldman House, 1997). ISBN 0-931674-32-8

Abstract of the Children's Book

This book is a beautiful story of love, hope, and the ability to believe that wherever the "next place" is for us in life (or death) holds the potential of being a place of contentment and joy.

Setting the Stage

1. Think about your own personal beliefs about what lies ahead for you, whether it is in a personal transition to a new home, new relationship, or the reality of dying.
2. Do you have a vision when you think of a "next place" in your life? How do you imagine it?

Notes on Reading the Book

The book should be read with optimism and sensitivity. The belief that we have the opportunity to share love and caring every day and to make that experience real, even when it means the loss of someone through death, is the point of this book.

Discussion Questions

1. How is *The Next Place* a book of hope and love? Does it only represent the beliefs of those who hold that there is another place after life?
2. In what ways can you talk with a student, or students, after the loss of a friend or loved one when it affects their daily lives? What words can you offer to help them work through their grief without imposing your own personal beliefs about what the next place is?
3. Does the emergency plan provide a means for follow-up after a loss or tragedy that will ensure that those for whom loss occurs will know that having feelings of fear, insecurity, loss, or grief are normal, even months to years after the loss? How can we ensure that we are following that plan?

Facilitating the Discussion

1. Elicit comments that the book is one of hope because it provides the opportunity to think that there is always a better day. This is true whether you see it as the tomorrow of our lives, or the belief that some have in an afterlife. It clearly can represent the next place in a move, change in position, home, or opportunity.
2. Help participants to discuss that, although their role as teachers is not to provide direct counseling, they are an adult contact for students. Their ability to read a student's emotions (heightened or flat) and to provide reassurance and, when needed, to recommend a counselor who can assist the student, is vitally important.
3. Have your emergency plan available to review or have a synopsis of the part that addresses the aftermath of tragedy for the school community. Make sure that everyone knows the plan and has the

opportunity to discuss ways that the plan might need to be amended or enhanced. If there is no plan for delayed response, discuss components to include in the plan.

Other Metaphorical Uses or Parallels

This book can be used to talk about transitions from middle to high school or high school to adulthood and can be a form of encouragement for living well each day and sharing with others.

Illustrations

The colorful illustrations are light and hope filled. It is possible to imagine that all is right with the world in these drawings and that ways of coping can be enhanced by just enjoying the "story" of the pictures.

Recommended Background Reading

D. Byrnes, "Talking with Children about Loss," *Childhood Education* 77, no. 2 (2000): 112.

Insight into Action

If the emergency plan for your school needs to be revised or developed because you have not included a "delayed" action plan, then either draft something for faculty discussion and acceptance or develop a plan with a committee of faculty.

DEATH, DIVORCE, AND LOSS: ACTIVITY 5

Purpose

The purpose of this activity is to discuss the ways that divorce impacts students and their learning and to help participants recognize the signs of student behavior that indicate potential home-based problems.

Materials

- Book: V. Lansky, *It's Not Your Fault, Koko Bear* (Minnetonka, MN: Book Peddlers, 1998). ISBN 0-916773-47-7

Abstract of the Children's Book

This is a read-along book for young children about divorce and the opportunity that parents have to teach their child (children) that the divorce is about the adults, not the child (children). Feelings of sadness and being mad are explored while both adults assure the child that the child is now, and always will be, loved by both parents and that they will always love him. The language provides good modeling for helping children to understand that divorce is not their fault.

Setting the Stage

1. How many students in your class (or in one of your classes) live with both biological parents? Do you know?
2. Have you seen signs of the effects of a divorce on one of your students? What were those signs?

Notes on Reading the Book

The book takes about ten minutes to read, but the language is helpful for teachers and others who might have to speak to a student about divorce. It is always best to involve the parent (or parents) and, when possible, a counselor should be involved. However, many schools do not have ready access to a counselor, yet teachers will encounter one or more students who have to deal with divorce or separation of a family through impending divorce. So, be sensitive to the voices that one would use to share the story.

Discussion Questions

1. Is it appropriate for a teacher to discuss divorce with a student? Is it easier to talk about divorce with a student if you can relate it to

a character such as the bear? Would it be easier to have the student read the book than to talk with him or her?

2. In the current age of "imposed" accountability, should teachers spend time discussing a student's reaction to divorce or separation?

3. What are some strategies that can be used in school to identify students who might need counseling due to divorce or separation?

Facilitating the Discussion

1. Help participants think through the importance of being sensitive to student reactions to divorce or separation and also to be aware of the limitations of their role in helping a student to cope with the situation. When counselors are available in the school, they should certainly be used. When they are not, you might want to discuss the position that you have set up in your school to address a student's response (e.g., contacting parent, recommending counseling).

2. While the ability to help students be successful in acquiring standards-based knowledge and skills is important, teachers must be sensitive to the individual student, particularly when they recognize changes in student behavior that might be a signal of family stress. Ensure that the discussion includes awareness of issues of confidentiality and personal confidences.

3. Research shows that some students will be extremely sad and show signs of depression and even sleeplessness. Anxiety levels peak if they feel they are going to be abandoned. They experience feelings of loneliness due to the loss of the other parent. If teachers are informed about the potential signs of stress on students relative to divorce or separation, help them strategize how they can support students and help them stay focused on their work.

Other Metaphorical Uses or Parallels

This book could be used for other forms of loss, such as death, although it is more difficult to help children understand when one parent is not available to them at all.

Illustrations

The illustrations are colorful and simple representations of family activities and how they look different when there are two homes for a child. The pictures do show caring adults who are trying to help the child understand that divorce is not about the child. There are helpful hints at the bottom of each page to facilitate discussion. This could be shared with parents who want to know how to help their child understand what is going on during a separation and/or divorce.

Recommended Background Reading

"Children and Divorce: Helping Your Children Cope" (www.bcm.tmc .edu/we_care/divorce.htm); "Divorce and How It Affects a Child" (http:// nh.essortment.com/divorcehoweffe_rhcq.htm); "Effects of Divorce on Children" (http://ut.essortment.com/effectsdivorce_rjqk.htm).

Insight into Action

Since teachers and staff are not immune to divorce themselves, it is important to help them think through their own feelings and emotions on this topic. Sometimes teachers need to think about how their own experiences may positively or negatively affect how they talk with their students. Using one or more of the sources in the background reading list as a talking point may help teachers generate discussions and ideas for helping students.

CHILD ABUSE AND NEGLECT: ACTIVITY I

Purpose

The purpose of this activity is to promote discussion and widen understanding about differing perspective of child abuse and neglect, as well as behaviors that are simply "bad parenting" or parental prerogative. Through this exercise, the many facets of abuse are explored, and the divergent interpretations as to what constitutes abuse and neglect are brought to light.

Materials

- Book: S. Well and S. Jeffers, *McDuff Moves In* (New York: Hyperion Books for Children, 1997). ISBN 0-7868-0318-5
- A copy of your state's laws regarding the reporting of child abuse and neglect, as well as a list of local resources for child and family support services

Abstract of the Children's Book

A lost white terrier survives a tumble out of a dog catcher's truck and spends a rainy night searching for a home. After much wandering, he smells something good to eat and is taken into Fred and Lucy's house where he is cleaned and fed. Lucy and Fred lament, however, that they cannot keep him. Instead of returning McDuff to the dog pound, they finally admit they want to provide him with a happy home.

Setting the Stage

1. Since state law varies, it is important that the facilitator determine, before the presentation of this professional development activity, which of the parental behaviors described in the survey found in appendix 1 would be actionable under state laws. Although the focus of this activity is not the legality of parental behaviors, a phone call to the area Department of Social Services or Child Protective Services will lend clarity from a legal perspective if participants are interested.
2. The survey (see appendix 1) should be photocopied and distributed to each session participant.
3. Participants keep their surveys in order to respond to the discussion questions that follow.

Notes on Reading the Book

A reader who is able to convey the sadness of the simple text using a slow cadence is the best type of reader for this story. It is important that the reader not rush; this is a book of relatively few words.

Discussion Questions

1. Is it abusive to leave a dog out in the rain overnight or to fail to provide shade for a dog in the summertime? Did you view McDuff as "abused" or "neglected" at the start of the story? Why or why not?
2. What questions on the survey, if any, are clearly child abuse, in your opinion? Why?
3. What behaviors are simply "bad parenting"?
4. Is there agreement among the group regarding which parental behaviors are simply different parenting styles, or behaviors that are a parental prerogative? Why?

Facilitating the Discussion

1. Have you heard students talk about, or witnessed yourself, parental behaviors that led you to question whether a child was being abused or neglected?
2. Make sure you are clear about how to report suspected abuse and/or neglect. (Review state guidelines and resources, noting where agencies, policies, and procedures are located.)
3. The Child Welfare League of America, a national child advocacy and protection agency, grew from the Society for the Prevention of Cruelty to Animals. In Boston in the 1800s, it was learned that although a child was being abused by his or her parents, there was, at that time, no laws forbidding the abuse of children. In desperation, local citizens had the parents arrested on animal cruelty charges, arguing that the child was a mammal and was therefore entitled to state protection. As we think about child abuse, is there behavior we tolerate when directed at children when, in general, we frown on animals being treated comparably?
4. Although there was some disagreement about what constitutes abusive behavior and what is simply "bad parenting," is there consensus among the teaching staff regarding how students ought to be treated while they are at school?

Other Metaphorical Uses or Parallels

This story could also be used to highlight the importance of family, or a place of belonging, for each and every child.

Illustrations

The story, based solely on the illustrations, is set in the 1930s. For history and art buffs, note the art deco flavor of the illustrations.

Recommended Background Reading

Abuse and neglect materials are available at www.mental-health
-matters.com.

Insight into Action

Is every adult member of the school community aware of the procedures for identifying and reporting suspected child abuse or neglect? How do members of your school community deal with borderline cases that are "bad parenting"? Is your school currently involved in, or a likely candidate for, providing classes on effective parenting for those who lack the necessary coping and parenting skills to deal with their children? Is there a need in your community for such services? If they already exist, are they well used?

Often school personnel are the "first line of defense" for defenseless children. In some communities, the rate of child endangerment is high; some parental misbehavior toward their children is commonplace and common knowledge. What can teachers do to avoid burnout in dealing with dysfunctional families? Are teachers' concerns taken seriously by the administration, the district office, and state policymakers? Have legislators become aware of the link between home behaviors and students' ability to learn? Who lobbies for children?

Ask for a voluntary school task force to review the adequacy of services to children, if the consensus of the group is that more needs to be done.

CHILD ABUSE AND NEGLECT: ACTIVITY 2

Purpose

The purpose of this activity is to foster the development of a "comfort level" for teachers to discuss the sexual abuse of children. The overall aim is to foster awareness of the widespread occurrence, signs, and effects of such abuse on children and young people.

Materials

- Book: O. Wachter, *No More Secrets for Me: Sexual Abuse Is a Secret No Child Should Have to Keep*, rev. ed. (Boston: Little, Brown, 2002). ISBN 0-316-99042-6
- 5×7 index cards and pens or pencils for each participant

Abstract of the Children's Book

In separate stories, the topic of child sexual abuse is presented in vignettes. The stories range in severity from an adult's lack of respect for a child's privacy and ownership of his own body to sexual molestation. Each of the children described in the stories is able to stop the abuse, often with the help of a trusted friend and/or adult. A synopsis of several stories follows:

"Talking Helps": A female babysitter doesn't respect a young boy's privacy or his ownership of his body. The boy expresses his concerns to his mother, who assures him she will deal with the babysitter.

"Just in Case": A girl at a video arcade is approached by a "grandfatherly" male who is frequently seen at the establishment. After he buys her a soda and tries to give her money, she is uncomfortable with his physicality with her. She says "No!" and reports his behavior to her mother. Greg, a boy at camp, is blackmailed by a camp counselor to remove his clothes under the threat that he'll be reprimanded for a minor misbehavior. Rather than comply, the boy leaves and informs the head counselor. Greg is assured that the problem will be resolved and not happen again.

"Promise Not to Tell": A girl tells her best friend that her stepfather has been fondling her. With the encouragement of her friend, the girl tells a trusted teacher, who assures her that the stepfather's behavior will stop.

Setting the Stage

1. Write a brief paragraph on a 5×7 index card regarding your gut reaction to the topic of today's professional development session.

This is to be done anonymously, then the cards are collected. While the book is being read, the facilitator should sort the cards into the following categories:

a. Anger and/or frustration
b. An attitude that makes light of or downplays the severity of the topic
c. A personal experience with abuse as a victim
d. A personal experience regarding abuse as a witness or confidante
e. A "societal perspective" on the severity or tragedy of abuse, including media
f. Concern about alleged abuse that was not substantiated
g. Commentary on services that are charged with investigating or prosecuting abuse claims, or other legal issues
h. Other (make a note about the topic)

Notes on Reading the Book

This book is too long to read in its entirety. A likely choice of vignettes to read are the first and the fourth, the first because it illustrates a child's attempts to claim ownership of his own body, and the latter because of its severity and the response of the teacher. The best reader for this book is one who has the maturity to give the topic the sensitivity it deserves.

Discussion Questions

1. Report to the group the breakdown by category of the responses to the Setting the Stage activity. What do the categories and the individual reflections within the categories tell us about this issue?
2. Did some of you have a hard time deciding what to write? Why was the assignment difficult for you?
3. How do personal feelings or "gut reactions" shape our ability to recognize, confront, and deal with this serious issue which we all *know* affects some students?
4. If any card(s) reflects a lack of seriousness, what do you suppose that means?
5. For those cards that report an encounter with abuse or an abuse victim, what is the overriding emotion that is conveyed?

6. Is the sexual abuse of children new, or is it simply that we hear more about it now?

Facilitating the Discussion

As questions are posed and answered, and as some of the content from the cards is shared, it may be helpful to interject some of the following information:

1. Stats on abuse claims and charges in your state and/or area
2. Upturn in abuse via the Internet
3. Prevalence of abuse across racial, ethnic, and socioeconomic lines
4. Reported versus actual cases of abuse
5. Typical legal response to substantiated abuse claims
6. Legal steps required of all teachers and school personnel regarding suspected abuse

Other Metaphorical Uses or Parallels

This book is unique in that its focus is to encourage discussions between parents and children regarding the types of and responses to abuse. The text could be used to facilitate discussions about the rights of children, parent–child communication, self-esteem, human rights, or as an exemplar of the diversity of topics about which school personnel must be sensitive.

Illustrations

This book is unusual in that the illustrations are secondary to the written content. June Aaron's illustrations are simple black line and crayon drawings that portray the same simplistic style across all four vignettes. They represent the hollow feeling one has in these circumstances.

Recommended Background Readings

Helpful information on child abuse and neglect is provided at the website: www.indianchild.com/child_abuse.htm.

Insight into Action

1. Look over the content of your curriculum. What is taught to students about the ownership and sanctity of their own bodies? If the topic is not broached, why is this topic omitted? What are district policies regarding conversations, particularly at the elementary level, about "good touching" and "bad touching"?

2. In addition to an examination of the curriculum, what services and programs are available in your area to assist children and families who are trying to cope with the aftereffects of abuse? Are teachers and other school personnel aware of these services? What relationships, if any, exist between these agencies and local schools? How can various organizations (social service agencies, schools, mental health organizations, law enforcement, child welfare agencies) better work together to combat abuse? What relationships exist between your school and such organizations?

3. What can be done to educate school personnel, streamline services, and encourage dialogue across the community about this problem and the need for solutions? In short, why, in your community, does child sexual abuse remain at epidemic proportions? Designate a point person in your school to spearhead the development of relationships with professionals across disciplinary and service area divisions. If we are to teach children they are to have no secrets, then the secret of child sexual abuse should not be kept by a community's adults. Make a commitment as a school community to keep the light turned on.

CHILD ABUSE AND NEGLECT: ACTIVITY 3

Purpose

The purpose of this activity is to discuss ways to identify and take action when a teacher believes a student is being abused or neglected.

Materials

- Book: B. Waber, *Courage* (Boston: Houghton Mifflin, 2002). ISBN 0-618-23855-7

Abstract of the Children's Book

This book is a short book with examples of all kinds of courage. Courage to try new things, courage to take risks, courage to stand up for what is right, courage to change behavior (self and others), and courage to do the right thing.

Setting the Stage

1. Think about a time that you had to deal with a difficult issue involving a student (e.g., a student confiding a difficult personal situation). How did you feel?
2. Do you have the courage to speak up when you see something that is wrong with (or hurting) another individual?

Notes on Reading the Book

The book should be read with confidence and expression that reflects the courage shown by each of the examples in the book. Voice inflection can clearly illustrate when courage is a function of trying something you want to do and experiencing some success (as the ice skater in the first illustration). Inflection can be used to show the hesitancy in some situations where courage is required (as the "night noise" page). Recognition of the importance of the courage of others (as in the example of the firefighter or police officer) can be expressed through body language that shows the relief we feel that there are those who provide that security for us. The final page gives the opportunity to show that courage comes from supporting others by an expression that enfolds the participants in the words (e.g., extending a hand and sweeping it in an arc in front of you to show that all of you are together.)

Discussion Questions

1. How was the courage that was expressed in checking the "night noises" like the courage teachers and administrators must have to address suspected abuse or neglect?

2. What are some of the things that would help you as a teacher to be more aware of the needs of students who are abused or neglected, particularly when it is not physically apparent?

3. Do you feel you are familiar enough with plan for addressing child abuse and/or neglect to act, or do you have ideas of ways that can better prepare ourselves and students to know they have a way to get help through school?

Facilitating the Discussion

1. Elicit responses from the teachers about the fact that "night noises" are representative of the "unknown." Teachers often feel ill prepared to deal with the unknown, particularly when it relates to the behavior of students. Encourage a discussion of how their professionalism in making a safe environment for students will/can lend itself to students knowing they can get assistance from them.

2. You might have a list of characteristics provided by a school counselor or from the website listed below which you have put on an overhead or large chart paper. Get teachers to add to the list or see if some might share examples of how they have seen one of the characteristics in their career. (Remind teachers not to identify specific students in their discussion).

3. In many states teachers are "required reporters" to state hotlines when they suspect abuse or neglect. Can teachers articulate state requirements in the group? Are they in your teacher handbook? Do members of the school administration remind faculty, periodically, about their responsibility to be observant and to report? If you do not have a plan, discuss ways that you could develop one for your school.

Other Metaphorical Uses or Parallels

Courage provides a great opportunity to discuss any number of issues about "doing right" in our schools. The daily opportunities to "do right" appear in needs of students, colleagues, parents, and community members. It sometimes takes more courage to act, or be supportive, or discuss issues, than to just walk away and pretend that one is not cognizant of the matter.

Illustrations

The illustrations in this book are stylized watercolors that beautifully represent the situation for which one needs courage. It is possible to point out in each one how the illustration represents the "type" of courage needed.

Recommended Background Reading

Abuse and neglect materials are available at www.mental-health -matters.com.

Insight into Action

Based on the discussion in question 3, you can revise your plan (or create it) and decide on a systematic way in which you will review or revise the plan. Additionally, you can provide periodic reminders to teachers that they are alert "eyes" and "ears" for the needs of their students and may be the most important link in helping a student connect with someone to address some negative events in his or her life.

❸

DIVERSITY

OVERVIEW AND BACKGROUND

For many educators, the ever-present reality of the diverse student populations served in public schools in America suggests that addressing diversity is a nonissue. However, the continuing achievement gap among groups, particularly tied to race, gender, and disabilities, suggests that it is crucial, as our schooling population continues to become more diverse, for educators to assess their own beliefs and consider their skills and abilities to educate students regardless of what they bring to the educational environment. The topics in this chapter address some of the more commonly recognized issues of diversity: disabilities, religion, affectional orientation, race, culture, ethnicity, and gender.

In most public schools in the United States, the number of students with disabilities being served in the general student population provides the greatest concern for educators. The majority of teachers have chosen and have been prepared to teach students through a general education (elementary, middle or high school) training program and in many states are not even required to have a course in educating students with disabilities. Given that students with disabilities have the only assurance under federal law that they will be provided a free, appropriate public education, and that guarantee comes in the form of a legally constituted document known as an individual education program (IEP), educators need to examine their own beliefs and perceptions about their role in serving these students. The activities provided under this topic will allow educators to consider some of the more prevalent disabilities, particularly ones that are not as visible as others, and will also help them consider their own understandings about their roles and the needs of students with disabilities.

Religion is addressed in this chapter as a means of engaging teachers in dialogue about some of the different aspects of various religious beliefs that students bring into the schooling environment. While public educators are well aware of their responsibility to separate religion from public schooling, they rarely have an opportunity to explore how their own religious beliefs affect their day-to-day decisions in the classroom and, likewise, how students' belief systems affect their day-to-day actions. It is not the intent of this topic to consider whether excluding religion from public schools is right or wrong, but rather to help educators think about their own beliefs and actions as they function in the school setting.

The decision to use the term "affectional orientation" was made with deep consideration for the growing body of literature that suggests that, even as early as elementary school, individuals who identify themselves as gay or lesbians express being aware that they are somehow different from their gender peers. Since sexuality is not within the purview of K–12 educational systems in America, it is not the intent of this topic to have educators discuss whether homosexuality is right or wrong, but rather to engage in discussions that help them consider their own behaviors as they relate to interactions with students and/or parents. The focus of these activities is on actions or reactions that ensure that every student has a safe environment at school regardless of his or her behaviors that may be perceived by others as being different from his or her peers.

In the most diverse society on the planet it seems almost incredible that there are still issues in our schools related to race, culture, and ethnicity. However, in many places the adults, in particular, have not participated in discussions about their own beliefs and perceptions related to the effects of race, culture, and ethnicity on the education of children and youth. While many schools have successfully adapted to the changing student populations and the multitude of races, cultures, and ethnicities represented therein, others have not. The activities in this chapter provide an opportunity for educators who have not had these discussions to share and learn from each other and to consider what they can and must do in their own schools to ensure that students can be proud of their heritage and celebrate their diversity.

Finally, this chapter provides activities to discuss issues related to gender. Although many would suggest that this topic is passé and that, in particular, girls and young women can do anything they want, the literature suggests that the number of girls and young women entering nontraditional fields for women is still only a fraction of the pool of talent among girls and young women. Although the activities for discussion on the topic of gender are focused on girls and young women, the reality is that the same behaviors that limit the expectations of girls and young women about what they can do also limit the expectations of boys and young men in considering roles that are not traditionally male. This chapter is intended to help educators discuss how various actions and behaviors on the part of educators and students may both positively and negatively influence the beliefs of students about what they can do based on their gender.

In the ever-increasing world of accountability, the need to examine the diversity of students in our schools and the needs of educators in serving them makes discussion of these issues imperative. The activities provided will serve as a starting point for dialogue among educators and can lead to a concerted effort to make sure that the individual needs of students, regardless of race, gender, disability, or affectional orientation, are being met.

TOPICS AND BOOKS DISCUSSED IN CHAPTER 3

Religion, 107-18
  In God's Name
  What Is God Like?
  Apple Pie Fourth of July
  Joseph Had a Little Overcoat
Affectional orientation, 118–28
  The Sissy Duckling
  Why a Disguise?
  Cracker the Crab and the Sideways Afternoon
Race, culture, and ethnicity, 128–47
  Satchel Paige
  The First Strawberries
  Isra the Butterfly Gets Caught
  I Love My Hair
  The Butterfly's Dream
  The Day of Ahmed's Secret
  Are You My Mother? ¿Eres tu mi mama?
Gender, 147-56
  Soul Looks Back in Wonder
  The Paperbag Princess
  Just Like Josh Gibson

DISABILITIES: ACTIVITY I

Purpose

The purpose of this activity is to examine the conscious and unconscious messages that are sent to individuals and groups depending on their place in the social hierarchy of schools.

Materials

- Book: J. Burningham, *Hey! Get Off Our Train* (New York: Crown Books for Young Readers, 1994). ISBN 0-517-88204-3
- Photocopies of the diagram of the triangle found in appendix 2

Abstract of the Children's Book

A young boy, in a dreamlike state, takes a journey on a model train with his "pajama bag dog." On his journey, he meets a variety of endangered animals, all of whom request passage on his train. Despite his initial reluctance and command to "Hey, get off our train," the boy accommodates all who climb on board. The group shares adventures, and, at the story's end, the boy finds himself back in his own bed. Much to his mother's surprise, however, their home is populated with the train's passengers.

Setting the Stage

On the handout in appendix 2, quickly place individuals and/or groups from your school in the category in which they belong based on the perception of membership in the in-group or the out-group. (Individuals may be those with or without power; groups may be formal or informal, as well as professional, community, or student.) Your determination of where to place individuals and groups should stem from your interpretation of an informal common consensus that exists in all complex organizations.

Notes on Reading the Book

This story contains a menagerie of emotions. The choice of reader should be based on someone who is not shy about conveying the emotions inherent in the text, for example, the pleading voices of the animals who desire passage on the train, the frustrated tones of a parent intent on getting her child to bed, the indignant voice of a train's engineer who orders uninvited passengers to "Hey, get off our train!"

Discussion Questions

1. What type of data (information) did you use to categorize individuals and groups?
2. Compare and contrast your lists. Are there common categories of people or groups that are clustered at one end of your hierarchical chart or the other?

3. Can you think of any individuals or groups who are so marginalized they didn't even make it onto the chart?
4. At the end of the book, before the boy returns to his bedroom, how does the train get unstuck?
5. What can be done in your school community to "move people up" to the top of, eliminate, or minimize the hierarchy?

Facilitating the Discussion

1. Some participants may be reluctant to acknowledge social cleavages in your school community. You may wish to prompt the exploration of these realities by asking participants if they've paid attention to the students' social cliques, to faculty or staff communication patterns, or to perceptions of hegemony, even within the larger educational organization (the District Office).
2. Even if they don't possess power or influence, which groups within your school *assume* they possess inherent superiority?
3. In the most communal of schools there still exist breakdowns in social equity. In this exercise, you are trying to help teachers and other staff recognize the subtle (or perhaps not so subtle) messages that the school "belongs" to some individuals or groups more than others. In many high schools, for example, student athletes are found at the top of the student pecking order; the uncool student factions (e.g., nerds, country kids, or those whose parents lack material wealth) are found at the bottom. Be sensitive regarding resistance on this topic. Although exclusionary practices often target varied subcultures, in too many schools, those routinely dismissed as "different" and therefore at the bottom of the hierarchy are students with special needs.

Other Metaphorical Uses or Parallels

This book can also be used to discuss racism, classism, gender, or any exclusionary practices. It can also be used to prompt explorations of conflict resolution, the thoughtlessness of bullying, and student ostracism through peer pressure.

Illustrations

Some of the illustrations are dark and ominous, lacking the cheery pastels of many children's books. Despite the threatening and oppressive tone of some pictures, particularly those of the train in motion, they are quite wonderful nonetheless. They inadvertently serve as powerful metaphors for how some students experience school. This book received a Parents' Choice Award for illustration in 1990. Part of this book's power comes from its illustrations.

Recommended Background Reading

J. H. Holloway, "Research Link/Inclusion and Students with Disabilities," *Educational Leadership* 58, no. 6 (2001): 86–88. This source includes an excellent reference list regarding research studies that address inclusion.

Insight into Action

The last line of the story regards the animals that inhabit the house. The boy's mother is asking him, "Does this have anything to do with you?" Teachers can be encouraged to inventory their own attitudes and behaviors regarding students with special needs. Do rumblings occur regarding efforts toward inclusion? What attitudes, if not overtly endorsed, are somehow tolerated? Does the teaching staff model for their students efforts to include *all* students and welcome the diverse gifts each student brings? If not, why not? Work with special education specialists who can help you brainstorm ways to bring students with special needs fully into the fabric of school life. All students, not just those with disabilities, will be better for it.

DISABILITIES: ACTIVITY 2

Purpose

The purpose of this activity is to highlight the importance of the inclusion of every student in the school community, and to differentiate the positives and negatives of categorizing students, particularly those with special needs.

Materials

- Book: I. Whybrow, *Sammy and the Dinosaurs* (New York: Scholastic, 1999). ISBN 0-439-23771-8
- Flip chart
- A variety of wide-tipped markers OR
- Overhead or computer on which you can compile the groups' responses

Abstract of the Children's Book

A boy named Sammy finds a box of toy dinosaurs in his grandmother's attic and immediately becomes attached to them. After he takes care of their basic needs, Sammy goes to the library to learn the proper names of each and every dinosaur. Despite his devotion to these toys (which he imagines are real), Sammy makes a mistake. Preoccupied, he leaves his dinosaurs on the train. Distraught, Sammy acts out and laments the loss of his special dinosaurs. His grandmother then takes Sammy to the train station to search for the missing dinosaurs. After proving his ownership of the dinosaurs to the lost and found man by calling each dinosaur by name, Sammy is reunited with his dinosaurs.

Setting the Stage

1. At the outset, inform the group that some material in this exercise is of a sensitive nature. Honesty is paramount, as is respect for the opinions and perspectives that are shared. In order for the exercise to be meaningful, frank participation is required.
2. Divide the group of participants in half and physically separate the two groups. Do not allow one group to see the instructions given to the other group.
3. Give the following instructions on a slip of paper to each member of the first, or the A group: "Make a list of the specific activities or tasks you or your colleagues use at the start of each school year to help students feel welcome and included in your classrooms."

4. Give the following set of instructions on a slip of paper to each member of the second, or B group: "Make a list of all of the groups of students that are readily identified by students and/or staff. Include both formal and informal groups, as well as groups that are commonly viewed in a positive or negative light."

5. After the first group completes the assignment, hand out the second set of instructions: "Place a star (*) next to every activity (if any) that includes mention or incorporation of students' names (e.g., at the high school level, looking over the class list to determine how to pronounce names; at the elementary level, making labels or name tags, labeling folders, desks, or cubbies for each individual student, etc.)." After the second group completes the assignment, hand out the second set of instructions for that group: "Place a (+) sign next to those group identifiers that the school community, in general, views positively. Place a (-) sign next to those that your school community views negatively. If you believe a group is viewed in a rather neutral light, do not mark it. However, most groups, like people themselves, are not viewed in a neutral way within school communities. Make a notation if you, personally, view a group differently than does the school community as a whole."

Notes on Reading the Book

The text contains many scientific names of dinosaurs, so the person reading this text must be comfortable pronouncing these names. The text also is rich in emotion, understatement, and complexity. The story is best read by someone with a dramatic flair, that is, someone who is comfortable whispering or shouting, as appropriate.

Discussion Questions

1. For Group A: Ask for members to share the activities or tasks they labeled with a star. Record those activities on a flip chart or overhead projector.

2. For Group B: Which groups were marked as negative? (It's okay for some of this to be funny; honesty and humor should be welcomed and encouraged.) Record these groups on a second list.
3. Ask why some groups are viewed in a negative light.
4. Did anyone in Group B mention "students with special needs" on either one of their lists? If so, why? If not, why not? What are the assumptions of placing students with special needs in a discreet group? What are the assumptions of assuming students with special needs blend into the student population as a whole?
5. For Group A: Ask why particular naming activities are important in making students feel valued and welcomed. What is the significance and power of an individual's name?
6. For the group as a whole: "To what extent are efforts of welcoming and recognizing the uniqueness of each individual, particularly those efforts to recognize students' names, offset by the group labeling that goes on in schools? After all, nothing is sweeter than the sound of one's own name.

Facilitating the Discussion

1. Does Sammy name or label the dinosaurs?
2. Naming implies a relationship. Labeling implies categorization. Think about conversations among school staff. Are labels used more often in your school than are names?
3. What role does Meg play in the story? Is there a Meg-like element in your school community? What can be done to expose and neutralize such negativity?
4. Sammy's relationship with the dinosaurs is one of reciprocity. How is this made evident in the story? To what extent, if any, is reciprocity of relationships encouraged in your school environment, particularly across group memberships? To what extent, if any, is communication encouraged across identified groups, particularly with those group members that are labeled as somehow different?
5. The dinosaurs are real and valuable only to Sammy. To what extent are members of identifiable groups, specifically special needs stu-

dents, marginalized and devalued within your school community? Why is this?

6. How might your school culture change if naming replaced labeling?
7. To what extent does caretaking elicit care? What opportunities are available for students to demonstrate an ethic of care to student peers?

Other Metaphorical Uses or Parallels

Despite its relatively simple premise, this book is rich in its illustrations and in the power of its simple message. This book could be used to spark conversations about wealth and value, either for things or for people. It could also be used to promote discussions of forgiveness and the permanence of relationships.

Illustrations

Note that the dinosaurs are real only after they have been taken care of by Sammy. Be sure to share the illustrations adequately; they're not to be missed, particularly their transformation from bent and broken to living friends. The magic of the illustrations in this book is conveyed not simply in the expressive faces of the central character, but also in the animation of the toy dinosaurs. Pay particular attention to facial expressions of the few adults in this story.

Recommended Background Reading

While this story is, on its surface, about friendship, on a deeper level it is about so much more: loyalty, perseverance, and the magic of childhood. It could also be used for professional development activities related to the importance of learning new things or self-esteem.

Insight into Action

Most of us do not choose our own names; instead, we bear the names given to us by our parents or guardians. Too often children do not choose the categories to which they are assigned or the labels that they wear. Does the school community strive to include children from marginalized groups into the mainstream of school activities, or do labels and categories persist in limiting opportunities for social, academic, and emotional interactions? Does your school have policies related to harassment of students with special needs? Are students afforded the opportunity to work with students who are disabled as peers, and not simply in a "helping" role? What opportunities routinely exist for reciprocity between given groups of students? How? Or why not?

DISABILITIES: ACTIVITY 3

Purpose

The purpose of this professional development activity is to help teachers and administrators consider the difficulties students with Asperger's syndrome have with social cues.

Materials

- Book: P. C. McKissack, *The Honest-to-Goodness Truth* (New York: Simon & Schuster Children's Division, 2000). ISBN 0-689-82668-0

Abstract of the Children's Book

This book focuses on a little girl and her lessons in learning the difference between telling the truth in a way that is hurtful and telling the truth in a way that is constructive and productive.

Setting the Stage

1. Give an example of a bright student who takes things literally, particularly social cues, and tell how.
2. Do you think all students are able to learn the value of social customs and mores?

Notes on Reading the Book

While the little girl in this story is able to learn the difference in telling the truth in a hurtful way and in a constructive way, individuals with Asperger's syndrome have a neurobiological condition that does not allow them to "process" the difference. Many can learn to "act" appropriately in certain situations, but will not read the "cues" in our society that lets them know whether a behavior is appropriate or not. As such, the best reader for this book is someone who can convey the affect and attitudes inherent in this story.

Discussion Questions

1. How is Libby's lack of awareness of her hurtful language in telling the truth similar to a student with Asperger's syndrome? How is it different?
2. In what ways can faculty and administrators provide support to students who have Asperger's syndrome and address the behaviors that the student is unable to discern as being inappropriate?
3. What plan can we develop in school that will help us address the needs of students whose behavior is a direct result of their disability?

Facilitating the Discussion

1. Libby was not trying to be hurtful, she was trying to do what she had been told, which was to "tell the truth." Because many individuals with Asperger's syndrome interpret social situations literally (and because it is often inconsistent with their cognitive abilities), they act like Libby did, but are unable to "understand," as she did, why it is wrong to be hurtful and to monitor that behavior and act more constructively.
2. In developing an IEP, the team members can identify specific strategies for helping the student get out of difficult situations. These might include a pass with every teacher for the child to go

to the guidance office when he/she is having a difficult time (or the teacher observes same), and so on.

3. Brainstorm ideas on how to resolve the conflict between enforcing the need for modified general school rules and consequences for a student with Asperger's syndrome (or any other disability) and decide on a way to implement the plan.

Other Metaphorical Uses or Parallels

This book can be used for discussions on values exploration. It can also be used to prompt a discussion of individual differences and communication problems and strategies, as well as the diversity of values and customs, particularly across cultures.

Illustrations

The illustrations provide a point for differentiating "normal" social understanding and Asperger's as Libby was able to show remorse for her "bluntness." It shows on her face. Talk about how that is different for a student with Asperger's syndrome.

Recommended Background Reading

Awareness of Chronic Health Conditions: What the Teacher Needs to Know (1995). ERIC Document ED415602; Bullard, H. R. "Ensure the Successful Inclusion of a Child with Asperger Syndrome in the General Education Classroom. *Intervention in School and Clinic* (2004). 39 (3), 176.

Insight into Action

Follow up on the action plan devised under discussion question 3 and review it periodically with teachers. Monitoring the effects of the plan on the targeted students through analysis of data (e.g., number of referrals for disciplinary action) can prove beneficial to ongoing support and development of appropriate student behavior.

DISABILITIES: ACTIVITY 4

Purpose

The purpose of this activity is to consider the humanity that is expressed when we think of individuals with disabilities as human beings and not as disabled people.

Materials

- Book: M. Shriver, *What's Wrong with Timmy?* (New York: Warner Books/Little, Brown, 2001). ISBN 0-316-23337-4
- Chart paper
- Markers

Abstract of the Children's Book

This book is written by the well-known reporter Maria Shriver, who is the cousin of a family member with disabilities. She provides a lovely framework of all the things that are loved by most children in our society without a focus on "how" a child views his or her world.

Setting the Stage

1. Think of something you have tried to do that you found difficult. What was it? Were you able to accept your limitations in your ability to do it?
2. What do you think about when you encounter a child who looks physically different (e.g., being in a wheelchair, having only one finger)?

Notes on Reading the Book

This is a powerful book about how we are alike and how we are different. The book takes about fifteen minutes to read, so you may want to read selected parts if you have limited time for discussion. You can actually tell the main part of the book by reading the first page and then the sentences that contain the large letter print. Read through it so that you are comfortable with the message. In private schools you may choose to read the part that has the sentence, "God makes all different types of children." In public schools, you may choose not to read this passage. You can still tell the story without it.

Discussion Questions

1. What is important to consider about the message of the book? Write down one or two ideas.
2. How do we, as adults, learn to accept people who look or act differently than those with whom we are most familiar or comfortable? Can we teach children acceptance if we do not model it?
3. In what ways can we as educators ensure that all students in school feel accepted and included?

Facilitating the Discussion

1. Give participants time to think individually and then to write down their ideas. Facilitate discussion about the value of seeing the strengths or gifts in others, rather than the limitations. Get participants to think about how we "label" individuals when we place a disability before their identity. For example, consider the difference in saying "the students with learning disabilities" instead of "learning disabled students" or "the students who are mentally retarded" instead of "mentally retarded students." Ask participants to think about why we use certain characteristics when we describe students and not others. That is, why do we use race or disability to describe people? Generally the most common reason is that we use it when people are different than we are. Encourage discussion to get people to the point that unless there is some expedient information provided by that descriptor, is the descriptor necessary in the first place?
2. Facilitate discussion here about the need to recognize our prejudices, misconceptions, and assumptions about others. Talk about the effect of focusing on individual's successes and strengths, rather than limitations.
3. Pair (or group) participants to brainstorm things that happen in your school and/or could happen that would model and reinforce

acceptance. After they have ten minutes or so to discuss this, have them post their ideas on chart paper. Then have someone from each group share the ideas and consolidate any duplicates.

Other Metaphorical Uses or Parallels

This book can also be used to discuss how participants can brainstorm ways to identify what skills students have and those they need to develop.

Illustrations

The illustrations are beautiful pastels that provide a lovely backdrop for a poignant story. The pictures should be shared by passing around the book or showing it during reading.

Recommended Background Reading

M. E. Block, "Americans with Disabilities Act: Its Impact on Youth Sports," *Journal of Physical Education, Recreation, and Dance* 66, no. 1 (1995): 28–33.

Insight into Action

You should follow up on discussion question 3 by posting the revised list on your teacher web pages or through hard copies to all teachers. After four to six weeks, revisit the list and see if others have ideas that can be added. Ask participants to share how they have seen the ideas working through their own behaviors or those of others.

RELIGION: ACTIVITY I

Purpose

The purpose of this activity is to help teachers explore how their own personal religious beliefs affect their teaching and interactions with students and other colleagues. Additionally, the discussion provides the opportunity for teachers to explore how public school personnel walk a fine line when considering their personal belief system(s), the belief system of individual students, and the U.S. Constitution.

Materials

- Book: S. E. Sasso, *In God's Name* (Woodstock, VT: Jewish Lights, 1994). ISBN 1-879045-26-5

Abstract of the Children's Book

This book is a parable where people seek to find the best name for God. It illustrates the desire for the individual to understand that the god of his or her belief is the only God. In the end the people come together and learn what God's name is.

Setting the Stage

1. Do your personal spiritual and/or religious beliefs affect your teaching? How?
2. Do your personal spiritual and/or religious beliefs affect your interactions with students? Colleagues?
3. Should you discuss religion with students?

Notes on Reading the Book

The reader for this book should be able to give equal expression to the different names given to God. The book should be read with expression and the illustrations shared to help the listener appreciate the diversity of opinions that exist surrounding what different individuals/groups use as the name for their god.

Discussion Questions

1. In our post-9/11 society, is religion more of a factor for people when they think about the educational issues Americans face? Why or why not?

2. Has religion become as much of a diversity concern as race has been in some parts of the country? How? What are the parallels?
3. Is there a need in school to consider religion as a factor in student development and interaction?

Facilitating the Discussion

1. Clearly since 9/11, more people think about the fact that there are people motivated, at least publicly, by religion in their attempts to destroy others who they view as the enemy. Students are affected because they fear the risk associated with threats to themselves and those they love, but do not always have much exposure to other religions to decide for themselves how much of the action is a part of the particular religion and how much is an individual or group acting in the religion's name. Public school educators, in particular, often find themselves in an awkward situation by trying to resolve questions or to have discussions for fear of appearing to promote one religion over another, which is a direct violation of the Constitution.
2. In some areas of our country, religious beliefs are extremely varied, and schools (e.g., charter schools) are being developed based on those religious beliefs. It may be important to develop an understanding among teachers and staff that for some religious groups, daily life decisions are more driven by their religious code than by the governmental codes (e.g., federal, state, and local laws).
3. Break teachers into random groups of three or four and ask them to identify strategies that they would use *if* the question of religion arose in their classes, or how they would address the death of a student whose religion was not of the predominant group (e.g., telling a second grader that a Jewish classmate "went to be with Jesus" because he thought the child would better understand it related to his own religion).

Other Metaphorical Uses or Parallels

The use of language to describe the characters in the book is valuable in discussing issues of racial and age diversity, such as the description of the farmer who is "dark like the rich brown earth" or the grandfather whose hair is "white with years."

Illustrations

The illustrations of both animals and human characters reveal much about the power of human beings to love, in spite of their differences.

Recommended Background Reading

R. Paige, *Guidance on Constitutionally Protected Prayer in Public Elementary and Secondary Schools* (2003). Available at www.ed.gov/policy/gen/guid/religionandschools/prayer_guidance.html (retrieved December 2003); Paige, *Secretary's Letter on Constitutionally Protected Prayer in Public Elementary and Secondary Schools* (2003). Available at www.ed .gov/policy/gen/guid/religionandschools/letter_20030207.html (retrieved December 2003).

Insight into Action

From discussion question 3, participants should submit their ideas for a listing to be reviewed at a subsequent meeting and/or posted to a website or online discussion group. Faculty/staff could come up with a frequently asked questions (FAQ) page, where ideas on responses to some commonly asked questions might be posted for all to review or access as needed.

RELIGION: ACTIVITY 2

Purpose

The purpose of this activity is to have a discussion among teachers regarding the sensitive nature of religion in public schools relative to student interests and curiosity (particularly among middle schoolers) and the importance of understanding what teachers should and should not do in participating in these questions/discussions with students.

Materials

- Book: K. L. Bostrom, *What Is God Like?* (Wheaton, IL: Tyndale, 1998). ISBN 0-8423-5118-3
- Chart paper
- Markers

Abstract of the Children's Book

Questions that children often ask about God are provided as if being answered by God. The book illustrates a child's curiosity and reveals some questions that educators may face as students bring some of the same questions into the school environment.

Setting the Stage

Think about this: You overhear several students discussing what God looks like. One student states God is a spirit, another says he is black, and yet another says no one knows. What would you do?

Notes on Reading the Book

Ask the participants to recall their curiosity as children about things they heard others discuss that were different than what they had been taught. Then encourage them to imagine themselves as the little boy in the story that you are going to share. Be sure that you share the pictures in a way that all can see. Encourage the participants to think about how a student might feel as he receives the answers to the questions.

Discussion Questions

1. Ask participants to write a short paragraph on how they would respond to a student who asks them questions similar to the ones posed in the book.
2. Break participants into random groups of three to four to brainstorm a list of questions that middle school students (or whatever

level you may have) might ask about religion. Have them put their questions on chart paper posted around the room.

3. Facilitate discussion about possible responses to the questions, being mindful to think through with teachers their responsibilities to separate church and state.

Facilitating the Discussion

Note: The discussion leader should be careful not to represent any particular religious view or personal religious positions.

1. For the short paragraph, it will be important for teachers to know ahead of time that they will turn the papers in (so submit anonymously) to allow all responses to be collated and posted.
2. Emphasize for this part of the discussion that they are the experts on middle school (or whatever level you may have).
3. Review the questions that were generated in discussion question 2 and clarify any language about which any participant may be unsure. Eliminate duplicate questions. Then brainstorm possible responses; ask someone to take notes.

Other Metaphorical Uses or Parallels

This book could be used to have community discussions on curricular issues related to teaching religion in public schools.

Illustrations

The illustrations provide insight into many human emotions and events, including sadness, mystery, and illness. The pictures capture children's wonder and curiosity about many aspects of life.

Recommended Background Reading

First Amendment Center, *A Teacher's Guide to Religion in the Public Schools*, Publication no. FO2A (Nashville, TN: First Amendment Center, 1999).

Insight into Action

The questions and possible answers should be made available as a resource for all teachers on the topic. There may be a need as a faculty to come up with a policy or clarify a practice that will be used in your school in response to such questions. For example, you might decide that on all questions of religion, you will have a stock reply: "That's a very interesting question and I encourage you to discuss it with your parents." Or perhaps there is agreement that you will have a means for teachers to turn in questions students express that will be added to your list. Faculty will then brainstorm possible responses in a future meeting and add them to your list or website. Another possible follow-up would be to generate a list of the questions and send them home to parents so that they can discuss their own personal beliefs with their children.

RELIGION: ACTIVITY 3

Purpose

The purpose of this activity is to discuss the appropriateness and feasibility of using the study of religions to teach morals, ethics, and honesty in public schools.

Materials

- Book: J. S. Wong, *Apple Pie Fourth of July* (New York: Harcourt, 2002). ISBN 0-15-202543-X

Abstract of the Children's Book

This story is about a little girl of Chinese heritage whose parents own a restaurant and she is sure that no one wants Chinese food on the Fourth of July. It portrays the tug of a first-generation American child who wants to honor her parents, sure that they do not understand Americans, and ends up being surprised at how "American" they are.

Setting the Stage

1. How many religious groups are represented in school?
2. Are religion and ethnic background inextricably linked?
3. Can one teach morals and ethics without including religious elements?

Notes on Reading the Book

This book is as "apple pie" as the Fourth of July and should be read with the enthusiasm a child has for this great celebration. This excitement is followed by disappointment when a child has to obey his or her parents but wants something different. Read the section on how slowly the day goes in a Chinese restaurant on the Fourth of July with a woeful, dragging voice. Then share the excitement of people showing up at the end of the day wanting something other than "traditional" Fourth of July "American" food.

Discussion Questions

1. As teachers, how can we honor the cultural diversity of our students that is more than just surface attention (e.g., an international day)? How can regular acknowledgement of the importance of a child's culture on who that child is be incorporated more fully into the school experience?
2. Where can we find adult individuals in the school community who can help us think through the effects on learning on children who are born in this country but whose parents came here from somewhere else (e.g., Mexico, China)?
3. In programs like Character Counts, are teachers able to tie the "lessons" to be learned to the importance of how we treat one another and how these same tenets are common across most religious beliefs?

Facilitating the Discussion

1. Here one should be facilitating the discussion on such issues as how cultural norms influence student behavior and, how some things (e.g., hard work) are valued differently in different social groups.

Likewise, moral/ethical issues such as honesty and integrity are taught and practiced across social levels, as well as religious groups, so the facilitator should be looking for acknowledgement of the individual actions of teachers on a daily basis to affirm a child's heritage, while helping him or her build good citizenship for the democracy.

2. It is important to find adult individuals who can interact with teachers to help them understand the values of the culture and what the adults of that community want for their children. For example, if you are in a migrant community and have Mexican families who are seasonal to your area, it would be helpful to go to the parents and see if you could find someone who could/would talk with a small group of teachers about what they teach their children and what they want their children taught relative to moral/ethical issues. This provides the opportunity for teachers to understand where they stand in relation to the parents and for parents to know that they are honored in the development of their children.

3. Teachers need to discuss the use of such programs as Character Counts relative to the underlying premises in the program. While most of these types of programs address values that are generally held among Americans, it is important to realize that, for some parents, they do not want these addressed in a formal way for their children and there may be a need for a discussion on how teachers expound on the concept if asked by students.

Other Metaphorical Uses or Parallels

This book could be used for a discussion about those seeking the Chinese food at the end of the Fourth of July. Why did they choose Chinese food instead of the more traditional food (e.g., hotdogs, potato chips)? This could lead to a discussion of how we are really more similar to each other and enjoy learning from other cultures, religions, or ethnic groups.

Illustrations

The illustrations are bright, colorful, "American pie" real for the Fourth of July, but the use of the Chinese heritage child reminds us that all of us come from different backgrounds and bring different strengths to the fabric of the society.

Recommended Background Reading

G. T. Sewell, "Religion Comes to School," *Phi Delta Kappan* 81, no. 10 (1999). Available at http://web4.infotrac.galegroup.com (retrieved December 2003).

Insight into Action

Follow up in one month (or less) with teachers through e-mail or an online discussion group to determine what opportunities teachers have had to apply the decisions made about how to address these issues with students. See if assistance is needed to provide support for any given teacher or group.

RELIGION: ACTIVITY 4

Purpose

The purpose of this activity is to discuss the effects of religion and religious observances in public schools. The focus of this activity is on understanding religious traditions.

Materials

- Book: S. Taback, *Joseph Had a Little Overcoat* (New York: Penguin, 1998). ISBN 0-670-87855-3

Abstract of the Children's Book

This story tells the tale of Joseph, an obviously poor Jew, who remakes his overcoat into a jacket, vest, scarf, handkerchief, and a button. Joseph's resourcefulness does not end, even after he loses his button. Joseph's is a tale of frugality and humor; it's also a song. Lyrics and music are printed at the end of the book.

Setting the Stage

1. Quickly write the names of religions or religious denominations about which you feel you know a great deal.
2. Quickly write the names of the religions or religious denominations represented in your school.

Notes on Reading the Book

While the story in this book is a strong, creative story, for the purposes of this activity, the emphasis should be on the various activities engaged in by the main character, Joseph. If you used this book in talking about the weight of poverty found elsewhere in this volume, emphasize the differences in this reading on the activities in which Joseph participated. Particularly note the clothing of the characters in the illustrations that represent the middle European, Jewish heritage of Joseph (e.g., the yarmulke). It will be important to move around so the book's illustrations can be seen by everyone, or use technology to facilitate viewing.

Discussion Questions

1. What representative items of the Jewish religion did you note in the illustrations in this book?
2. How were the activities in which Joseph participated similar to ones in which you participate? Different?
3. Is there a need for religious awareness in school? How? Why?

Facilitating the Discussion

1. The facilitator may need to mention some of the representative items: the yarmulke on the men, the menorah on the table in the illustration with his vest, "mozl tov" on the wall in the picture with his handkerchief, or the newspaper with a headline about the rabbi on the page with the little button.
2. Elicit responses for similarities between participants and the book's protagonist, such as visiting family and friends, singing in the chorus, working around the house, and going to his nephew's wedding. Differences might be things like the ethnic costumes worn, the type of dances, and so on.

3. Elicit responses that address the need to accommodate student religious observances that take them from school. Emphasize the need to address the establishment clause of the Constitution, which forbids the establishment of religion by the state, but the requirement in a democracy to respect the beliefs of others.

Other Metaphorical Uses or Parallels

This book can be used to address the issues of poverty (see the weight of poverty section in this book), as well as creativity.

Illustrations

The illustrations are colorful, bright, and lyrical. For the purposes of this activity, focus on the illustrations and how they represent one's religious beliefs even when the story is universal. The pictures contain fragments of Jewish life and culture. Pay special attention to the cutouts that predict the newest transformation of Joseph's overcoat and the activities to which he wears the piece.

Recommended Background Reading

K. Schilbrack, "Religious Diversity and the Closed Mind," *Journal of Religion* 83, no. 1 (2003): 100–108.

Insight into Action

Determine the interest of the participants in having further discussions or engaging in a book reading that will help all members of the faculty to better understand and accept the religious diversity represented in the school, community, and the culture at large. Books that could be shared are listed under recommended background reading.

AFFECTIONAL ORIENTATION: ACTIVITY I

Purpose

The purpose of this activity is to help teachers consider their roles in student interactions that are reflective of sexual identity development. A teacher may well be the person to whom a student turns for advice when trying to work through his or her sexual identity.

Materials

- Book: H. Fierstein, *The Sissy Duckling* (New York: Simon & Schuster Books for Young Readers, 2002). ISBN 0-689-83566-3

Abstract of the Children's Book

This book is the story of a duckling who enjoyed cooking and playing with puppets when other male ducklings were playing football, and the challenges he faced with his father over his personal interests. In the end, he manages to save his father's life and his father realizes that the most important thing in a relationship is not about the interpretations we make about another person's interests, regardless of the gender stereotype tied to that interest, but rather in the character of the person.

Setting the Stage

1. Are there issues that arise in school about the affectional behaviors of students?
2. Are behaviors that display affection acceptable in your school (e.g., holding hands, carrying each others books, telling others they are a couple)?
3. If any or all of these behaviors are acceptable, does it differ for you if the students are of the same gender?

Notes on Reading the Book

This book is not specific to gay or lesbian issues in our society, but does provide a framework for considering the stereotyping that is done by adults about what is "female" and "male" behavior. When reading this book, it is important not to convey a perceived stereotype of the duckling when his behaviors seem "out of character" for his gender. Make sure that the reader reflects the genuine interest the duckling has in the activities as an individual without regard to gender.

Discussion Questions

1. If you imagine the duckling as a student you know, are there students who exhibit interests in activities that are not "typical" or "expected" of his or her gender in school? in the community? in this country?

2. Does the school have a policy on public display of affection (e.g., hand holding, kissing)? Do you think most teachers presuppose that all students are heterosexual and therefore address these issues in terms of "boys and girls?"

3. What resources does the school or community have in place to provide support for students who are seeking help and understanding of their affectional or sexual identity?

Facilitating the Discussion

1. The purpose of this discussion question is to help teachers and administrators consider their behavior relative to students when they make certain activities "male" and others "female." While this behavior on the part of adults in schools does not necessarily relate specifically to students who have identified themselves as homosexuals (e.g., it may limit a student in exploring an area of learning or growth in which she or he may excel), but it may be particularly confusing for a student who is struggling with his or her affectional or sexual identity.

2. Often teachers and administrators limit their observations of acceptable and unacceptable public displays of affection to heterosexual couples. There may well need to be discussions among faculty, depending on your community norms and values that address those same behaviors when exhibited by same sex students, as well.

3. Brainstorm a list of resources in the school or community where students can be directed when issues of social/personal interactions, particularly among adolescents, can be directed. You may have a highly qualified counseling staff in your school, or may need to identify community resources.

Other Metaphorical Uses or Parallels

This book can also be used to address the differences in creativity and intelligence among students in your school. For example, the fact that the duckling liked to cook may be important for people to consider as a career issue, without attributing gender to the talent or interest.

Illustrations

The illustrations are colorful and boldly portray the duckling's interests and talents without making him look "sissy." However, the reaction to his interests, as unacceptable to his father, is evident in the posture and look on the faces of the other ducks.

Recommended Background Reading

Affectional and sexual orientation study guide published by the Human Rights Education Association. Available at www.hrea.org/learn/guides/lgbt.html.

Insight into Action

Provide a vehicle (e.g., post a discussion group online) that allows teachers to explore their own ideas and feelings on this topic. Do provide ground rules that the purpose of this activity is to examine your role as school personnel, not to change each other's personal views on the issues of homosexuality. Many individuals need time to think about their roles and responsibilities, particularly when they are in conflict with their personal beliefs. It will be important to identify a staff member who can be objective and monitor the site for inappropriate use of the discussion group.

AFFECTIONAL ORIENTATION: ACTIVITY 2

Purpose

The purpose of this activity is to illustrate the "invisibility" of heterosexuality and promote an understanding of the difficulties gay, lesbian, bisexual, and transgendered persons face in efforts to be who they are, particularly in contexts that have been historically hostile to them, such as schools. Note: This is one of the few professional development activities in which you will get more honest input if the program is described simply as "diversity."

Materials

- Book: L. Numeroff, *Why a Disguise?* (New York: Simon & Schuster Books for Young Readers, 1996). ISBN 0-689-80513-6

Abstract of the Children's Book

This book presents scenarios in which a young boy benefits from wearing a disguise in order to avoid unpleasant events, such as taking a bath, meeting up with the school bully, and eating lima beans. By the story's end, the boy appreciates taking the mask off, as "at the end of the day, it's nice to know that you're still you."

Setting the Stage

Note: There are two separate Setting the Stage activities for this program. Have the participants complete the first activity before you introduce and conduct the second Setting the Stage activity.

1. Make a list of the top five descriptors (adjectives, roles, or memberships) that you use to describe yourself to yourself. Think of this as your "self-identity" list. Keep this list; you needn't show it to anyone else.
2. As you look around the room, what inferences can you draw from your coworkers based only on their physical appearance? Make a list of descriptors (without using the person's name) of what you see and infer (e.g., "a woman probably dyes her hair, as I can see the roots are a different color than the rest of her hair" or "a young man probably exercises regularly, as he is trim and muscular"). Include at least one inference on at least ten different people. Without putting your name on the paper, turn it in to the activity's facilitator.

Notes on Reading the Book

This text is fairly short; be careful not to rush through the text and illustrations. The person who reads the book should take the topic of this professional development activity seriously. The individual who facilitates this activity should be sensitive to, and empathic about, the concerns of gay, lesbian, and bisexual people.

Discussion Questions

Note: There is no handout for the discussion in this activity.

1. Begin to read, in random order, the lists that were written by the participants. Ask the group if anyone wishes to "claim" each descriptor as it is read. Note: Keep this activity light; some of the descriptors may draw laughter. This is to be encouraged. Keep this activity moving; if no one claims a descriptor, move on to another item. You needn't read every list in its entirety, but read at least as many descriptors as there are participants.
2. When you have finished reading the list of descriptors, ask participants to raise their hands if none of the descriptors matched the first list they made (their self-identity lists). Conversely, ask if anyone had a match between how they think of themselves (from the self-identity list) and the descriptor lists.

Facilitating the Discussion

Pose the following questions to participants:

1. Does everyone wear what might be considered a costume?
2. Do the physical elements about which one has control (e.g., clothing, jewelry, hairstyles, makeup) illuminate or hide who a person "really" is? What about you? Are you particularly proud of some of the roles that you play? (For example, if you listed "husband," do you wear a wedding ring? If you listed "mother," do you have pictures of your children in a locket?)
3. For those participants who seem proud to claim a descriptor, probe as to why they claimed ownership. Without putting them on

the spot, ask if the descriptor in any way matches any items on their self-identity list.

4. For the less-than-flattering descriptors, were you reluctant to claim them as a personal match? Why is that?

5. Even if no one described you according to the self-identity list you produced, do you share with others how you define and think about yourself and the roles that you assume?

6. Ask if anyone is willing to share their self-identity list. Ask the individual, and the group, how the individual might demonstrate that self-descriptor. Is it important to be able to authentically be who you are?

7. What might it be like if that most important self-descriptor had to be hidden from much of society?

Other Metaphorical Uses or Parallels

This book could be used for any diversity-related issue, such as is often the experience for people who are gay, lesbian, or bisexual, to discuss discrimination and bigotry. It could also be used as a metaphor on the results of peer pressure.

Illustrations

The book is illustrated by David McPhail, an illustrator of many children's books. Pay attention to all of the book's characters' responses to the disguise. (Most look disgusted or confused.)

Recommended Background Reading

S. Wessler and W. Preble, *The Respectful School: How Educators and Students Can Conquer Hate and Harassment* (Alexandria, VA: Association for Supervision and Curriculum Development, 2003).

Insight into Action

Ask participants to keep a mental journal of the assumptions they make about parents and students based on their appearance. Promote reflection on how those assumptions may shape the type and quality of interactions that take place between teachers and the publics they serve. Are those assumptions based on stereotypes, or on the positive self identifiers the individual probably holds?

AFFECTIONAL ORIENTATION: ACTIVITY 3

Purpose

The purpose of this activity is to help participants consider the importance of acceptance of individual differences even when it appears to challenge the norms of the group. Students bring many diverse interests and abilities to school and there is a need to help teachers address those that are specific to the expressed affectional orientation of some students or parents who visit your school.

Materials

- Book: M. Cogdill, *Cracker the Crab and the Sideways Afternoon* (Simpsonville, SC: Two Bear, 2002). ISBN 0-9725560-0-1

Abstract of the Children's Book

This book shares the beautiful story of a crab who is trying to determine his identity and how he fits into the world in which he lives. He is aware that others move along different paths than he does but not sure how to make himself move in the same way. He even finds evidence of a straight path, which turns out to be caused by a wheelchair, and realizes the beauty in everyone.

Setting the Stage

1. Although educators often feel that discussions about affectional or sexual orientation are not appropriate, have you thought about how you feel (or would feel) when meeting with a student's parents who are of the same gender?

2. Can you be objective about a student's educational needs when you sit across a table from a student's parents who are of the same gender?

Notes on Reading the Book

This book should be read with some recognition of the crab trying to figure out where he fits in the world and why his sideways movement is different from others. Read part 1 with curiosity for what the crab anticipates he'll find in following the straight steps between the two lines he expects were drawn for him. In part 3 read the struggle of trying to find his way and then meeting someone who helped him see that life is full of connections.

Discussion Questions

1. How can the movements of the sideways crab be related to stereotypes many have about sexual or affectional orientation?
2. Are there reasons to be aware of a student's affectional orientation? How should a teacher deal with this?
3. What needs do we have in school for helping faculty and staff to be accepting of a student's and/or parent's affectional orientation?

Facilitating the Discussion

1. Help faculty think through the stereotypes that are portrayed about effeminate behaviors, particularly of males, and masculine behaviors of females, that result in some people making judgments about their affectional orientation. The sideways movement described for the crab and the response to it should help participants to think about ways that individuals show a lack of acceptance of individual differences.
2. Elicit responses that address the circumstances where issues of affectional orientation can arise, for example, school dances, certain assignments given in classes (e.g., the biggest issue you've faced in life), teasing of students even when one's orientation is *not* known. Talk through strategies that you have in your school to address

these issues. For example, you may have a counselor who is particularly trained to discuss these issues with students, or you may have a standard response about the need to discuss such issues with one's parent or religious adviser but that it's not appropriate, regardless of one's orientation, to discuss this.

3. Often teachers have not considered the fact that there are students whose parents are a homosexual couple and that they will both be involved actively in the student's life. If teachers have not thought about this possibility, it is highly probable that when meeting parents of the same gender, they will react in such a way as to place a barrier between the parent(s) and teacher relative to the student's educational program. It is important for teachers to know that you are not asking them to accept or even condone the relationship, but rather to realize that as professionals they are charged with accepting parents and students in their educational responsibilities for student learning.

Other Metaphorical Uses or Parallels

This book can also be used to discuss disabilities and the reactions that some people have to those who look different or behave differently.

Illustrations

The illustrations are beautiful depictions of the ocean and shore and provide an orientation to the challenges that the crab experiences in trying to determine and accept his personal identity.

Recommended Background Reading

J. A. Banks, "On Educating for Diversity: A Conversation with James A. Burke," *Educational Leadership* 51, no. 8 (1994): 21–31.

Insight into Action

Create a book reading, using the article mentioned in the recommended background reading above, and have a counselor or someone from outside your school discuss the ways that teachers can show acceptance and understanding of the lives of others.

RACE, CULTURE, AND ETHNICITY: ACTIVITY I

Purpose

The purpose of this activity is to examine the personal determination that allows individuals to succeed even when they are not members of the dominant culture. This can be evidenced regardless of race, culture, or ethnicity.

Materials

- Book: L. Cline-Ransome, *Satchel Paige* (New York: Simon & Schuster Books for Young Readers, 2000). ISBN 0-689-81151-9
- Sticky notes
- Paper and pencils for each participant

Abstract of the Children's Book

This book tells the story of a young boy's determination to play baseball. Even though he suffered the effects of poverty and crime, he kept his sights on his goal. The result of his determination and support from those who believed in him was that he became the first African American baseball player to be inducted into the Baseball Hall of Fame.

Setting the Stage

1. Think about a time when someone about whom you care (child, parent, and sibling) had an all-consuming goal. What was that goal? Did he or she obtain it?
2. Who should decide which goals for an individual are the "right" goals?

Notes on Reading the Book

Approximately fifteen minutes are needed to read the entire narrative. The language is certainly descriptive and worthy of reading, but depending on time available for the discussion, it might be best to just tell the story through the pictures. There are some particular passages such as his "trouble ball" or "bee ball" where you might want to read the actual paragraph. (Use sticky notes to mark those passages that you want to use the language of the writer.)

Discussion Questions

1. Was there justification, in Satchel's mind, for why he stole? Do you think that your students who have stolen think that their actions were justified?
2. Do you think that stealing is unique to a given group of people? By race? Socioeconomic group? Why or why not?
3. What impact does the desire to attain a goal have on a student's determination? What if the goal is contrary to the values of the community (e.g., not to do well in school)?

Facilitating the Discussion

1. Satchel stole to ensure that there was enough money for food for his family. This probably justified his behavior in his mind, but the result was that he got caught and had to pay the price by being sent to "reform school." Ask participants to discuss examples of students (without names) who may have had similar circumstances and who either got caught or punished (or didn't). How did they feel about this as they matured?
2. It is important here for participants to really talk about the fact that people steal for different reasons: some for survival, some for greed (mention the corporate CEOs of the late 1990s and early 2000s). Clearly stealing is a social behavior and not one that is promoted or condoned by any specific group, regardless of race, culture, ethnicity, or socioeconomic status.
3. Ask participants to examine the positive effects of reform school on Satchel's life. How can this compare to their roles as teachers in helping students to focus on a goal and work hard? Do they help students work hard when the response to failure to perform is an F rather than a helping hand to ensure that the student *will* achieve?

Other Metaphorical Uses or Parallels

This book can also be used to talk about the value of hard work and achievement for any individual.

Illustrations

The illustrations are evident of the struggles that Satchel faced. The first page provides an incredible depiction of the poverty in which Satchel lived (such as the rag in the window). The illustrations of his form in pitching and batting are evident of the passion he exhibited for his sport.

Recommended Background Reading

K. J. McKenzie and N. A. Crowcroft, "Race, Ethnicity, Culture, and Science: Researchers Should Understand and Justify Their Use of Ethnic Groupings," *British Medical Journal* 309, no. 6950 (1994): 286–88.

Insight into Action

Follow up with participants two to three weeks after the discussion to solicit ideas for ways that they have found to guide students to more successful achievement. Ask them to identify ways that they have considered to help students focus on their personal goals and how school can help them achieve them. Share these ideas via e-mail or a listserv or a hard copy for each teacher.

RACE, CULTURE, AND ETHNICITY: ACTIVITY 2

Purpose

The purpose of this activity is to explore the influence of culture on student belief systems and ways to honor that while exploring the views of others.

Materials

- Book: J. Bruchac, *The First Strawberries* (New York: Puffin, 1998). ISBN 0-8037-1331-2

Abstract of the Children's Book

This book tells the Cherokee tale of how important it is to resolve differences and not let anger blind us to the beauty in our world. It further illustrates how the willingness to forgive results in healing.

Setting the Stage

1. Think about the last time you had a difference of opinion with someone that resulted in anger or avoidance of the other person. How significant was the issue on which you differed?
2. When you disagree with a student (e.g., over behavior), do you work to resolve the difference or do you just "send the student to the principal" and when she or he returns ignore the problem?

Notes on Reading the Book

This is a tale that should be told with consideration for the tribal nature of storytelling. The reader should be relaxed and comfortable and should make every effort to "tell" the story versus reading it.

Discussion Questions

1. How was the difference between the husband and wife much like the differences that educators experience with each other? Why?
2. What did the woman miss by being blinded by her anger? Are there examples of how we are blinded by anger in education (e.g., not understanding why students like certain music, legislative mandates, or new district policies)?
3. How do things change for the woman when she is forced to open her eyes? How can the leaders among us help open our eyes to the issues we face in serving students who have different values from our own?

Facilitating the Discussion

1. Because educators spend so much time together in a school (often more time than they have to spend with their families on a day-to-day basis), the closeness often clouds our ability to look at the differences we bring to the environment. Thus, we often let disagreements grow rather than try to address them and resolve them.

2. The woman missed the beauty of the strawberries because her anger kept her from being observant. Discuss ways that teachers react when they don't understand the differences in a student's culture or related legislative mandates. Discuss ways that we could address the concerns without rising to the level of anger.

3. When the woman finally sees the strawberries, she realizes that she wants to share and that she needed to make her needs known, as well. By taking on the responsibility, whether as teacher or administrator, to resolve differences and learn from others, we can find ways to improve schools and schooling for all students. Brainstorm ways that you can celebrate differences among students and faculty.

Other Metaphorical Uses or Parallels

This book can also be used to help students understand the effects of different cultures on a student's views.

Illustrations

The lovely illustrations are soft and muted and bring to life the beauty of the environment, as well as the reality of its loss when the woman and man act on their anger instead of their love.

Recommended Background Reading

Race, culture, and ethnicity in education are covered extensively in the Harvard University Fellows program on the same topic. Available at www.gse.harvard.edu/news/features/postdoc09012001.html.

Insight into Action

Either use a committee or encourage teams or departments to find ways to celebrate the diversity in your school and/or community beyond what you are already doing. Find ways to get media coverage of these events and involve the community for the enhancement of all involved.

RACE, CULTURE, AND ETHNICITY: ACTIVITY 3

Purpose

The purpose of this activity is to have participants consider the beauty that each student and adult brings to the school environment and to find ways to celebrate those unique aspects.

Materials

- Book: C. Young-Robinson, *Isra the Butterfly Gets Caught for Show and Tell* (Columbia, SC: Yoroson, 2001). ISBN 0-9706985-0-X

Abstract of the Children's Book

This book tells the story of a beautiful young butterfly that is captured and taken to school for show-and-tell. Although the butterfly had been warned of the dangers of being captured (and taken to school) she ended up being caught by a little girl, Miya. Her experience at school is that she was admired and then set free. Her day in show-and-tell created a memory she remembered forever.

Setting the Stage

1. For how many of your students can you identify their race, culture, or ethnic ties?
2. How much do you know about the different aspects of those students' heritage?
3. What concerns do you think parents have about sending their children to school when they have strong ties to a culture that is different from the dominant school culture?

Notes on Reading the Book

The book can be read as a folktale with the beauty of nature being expressed in the description of the butterfly, Isra. The voice of the mother butterfly can express the concern that all parents have in sending their child out into the world. The concern of imprisonment and the unknown can be expressed when Miya catches Isra. Finally, Isra can express the contentment of acquired knowledge when she shares her "show-and-tell" experience with her family.

Discussion Questions

1. In what ways are the concerns of the mother butterfly similar to parents of students in school when they send them to us to be educated?
2. In what ways do you honor the culture and traditions of individual students in your class(es)?
3. In what ways do you think we could more fully and genuinely honor the culture and traditions of our students?

Facilitating the Discussion

1. Elicit responses that address the conflict that some parents have because of strong cultural or religious beliefs when they send their child to public schools. For example, parents might be worried that the child may be ridiculed; that the child may be disadvantaged if teachers do not understand the cultural differences, such as clothing; or that the child may express beliefs in response to questions in class that will result in prejudicial behavior on the part of others.
2. Ask teachers to write down one or two things that they do in class to allow students to verify and express their cultural or ethnic heritage. For example, a middle school English teacher may have students interview an older family member on some aspect of his or her life when studying Alex Haley's *Roots*.
3. In pairs or groups of three to four, ask teachers to generate ideas of ways that they can share the culture and ethnicity of students on a regular basis and incorporate it into the ongoing instruction in their classes.

Other Metaphorical Uses or Parallels

This book could also be used to discuss issues related to religious differences and their effects on the culture of schooling. When students wear the clothing of their religion (e.g., Muslims) in a mainstream school, it is important for others to understand the basis for that clothing and acceptance of the rights of students to dress in the tradition of their family beliefs.

Illustrations

The illustrations are simple colorings that tell the story of the butterfly through color and muted tones of the surrounding world.

Recommended Background Reading

Race, culture, and ethnicity in education are covered extensively in the Harvard University Fellows program on the same topic. Available at www.gse.harvard.edu/news/features/postdoc09012001.html.

Insight into Action

From the information gathered in discussion question 3, create a list of ideas that can be shared among teachers. Consider having a group of teachers and parents and/or community members who can address ways that the faculty and students can celebrate the diversity within the community and acknowledge their commonalties.

RACE, CULTURE, AND ETHNICITY: ACTIVITY 4

Purpose

The purpose of this session is to demonstrate the multifaceted notions of beauty that shape students' self-esteem, with a special focus on African Americans.

Materials

* Book: N. A. Tarpley, *I Love My Hair* (Boston: Megan Tingley, 1998). ISBN 0-316-52375-5

Abstract of the Children's Book

Kenyana, the story's narrator, explains the joys and pains of her hair, the powerful memories associated with her hair, and the lessons she learned from her mother about her hair's beauty and symbolic value.

Setting the Stage

1. Think back to your childhood. Can you remember how, or from whom, you learned about what is physically beautiful? If you have a hard time remembering how those seeds were planted, why do you suspect that is so?
2. If you can remember your early experiences about discovering the meaning of physical beauty, why do you suspect the memories remain after all of these years?
3. From where or from whom did you learn about the quality of your physical appearance? What feedback did you get from significant others about how you looked?
4. To what extent, if any, was the feedback you received about your physical appearance as a child reinforced by the norms of beauty prevalent in American society at the time?
5. (This is to be written on a piece of paper and held by the writer in confidence for his or her own reflection later in this exercise.) The first rule of being human is said to be "You will be given a body. You may love it or hate it, but it is yours for the duration this time around." How did social norms contribute to your learning to love or hate your own body? Which of those social norms do you still hold to today? Is there any congruence between how you view your body and how you define yourself from a cultural or ethnic perspective?

Notes on Reading the Book

This text's narrator is an African American girl. A reader who is comfortable emoting the many, sometimes conflicting, emotions present in the text is the best choice to read this book aloud.

Discussion Questions

1. The story's narrator reports deeply conflicting emotions about the value and beauty of her hair. Do your responses to the questions posed at the beginning of this activity reflect similar ambiguity? Did aspects of your own physical appearance not "fit" with prevailing social norms?
2. Kenyana's teacher and mother do much to encourage an acceptance of and gratitude for her hair. Is hair *really* that important to Kenyana? How do your responses to the first three questions of this activity shape your response to this question?
3. To what extent, if at all, did your own lessons about what is physically beautiful reflect the values of the dominant culture in America?
4. To what extent, if at all, does this matter to you? To the community of which you are a part? To students in your classrooms?

Facilitating the Discussion

Note: It may be helpful to read the author's note at the beginning of the text to begin this discussion. It may be important also to use humor in this activity, for it asks participants to divulge personal memories and feelings about their own physical appearance.

1. For some participants, asking them to reflect on how they learned about what is beautiful may result in frustration. This may be because ideas about something as powerful yet seemingly invisible as "beauty" are extremely subtle. It's not that we are not taught about what is beautiful, but rather the lessons are deeply embedded in myriad aspects of life; as such, it can difficult to articulate because they are both ever present and seemingly benign.
2. Clearly, the issue is not simply one of physical appearance, but rather how our feelings about our physical attributes contribute to

a sense of self. For adolescents in particular, this can be a deeply painful subject. Only by reminding teachers of the powerful lessons they may have experienced as children will some understand the power and value of their students' physicality as regards their self-acceptance.

3. Finally, with regard to question 5 in the Setting the Stage activity, ask participants to reflect on their response to that question in terms of the messages that they may convey to students about the value of their bodies, the importance of their physical appearance, and the tool that the body is for personal, ethnic, and cultural expression.

Other Metaphorical Uses or Parallels

This book may be used to promote discussions of the importance of family and role modeling, self-acceptance, and cultural diversity.

Illustrations

The large watercolor illustrations by E. B. Lewis celebrate the powerful message of this book. They not only capture the meaning of the text, they amplify it. As such, it is imperative that the reader take time for participants to appreciate the illustrations.

Recommended Background Reading

Y. Choi, *The Name Jar* (New York: Random House Children's Books, 2001); K. Kissinger, *All the Colors We Are* (St. Paul, MN: Redleaf, 1994); S. M. Nieto, "Profoundly Multicultural Questions," *Educational Leadership* 60, no. 9 (2002–2003): 6–10; N. A. Tarpley, *Testimony: Young African-Americans on Self-Discovery and Black Identity* (Boston: Beacon, 1994).

Insight into Action

Perhaps some of the men who participate in this exercise have a hard time fully comprehending the power and importance of appearance, particularly those attributes that reflect the values of the dominant culture. On an electronic discussion board, continue this discussion with a focus on beauty, gender differences, and ethnicity. Do girls and women receive more messages than do men and boys about the value of their physical appearance? Are social norms more conflicting for minority women than for minority men? How has this changed in the past decade?

Also, pay particular attention to how activities and symbols, as well as learning materials, reflect values of a dominant culture at your school. Do an audit of everything that is posted in your school with a focus on the ethnic or cultural values imbedded in the displays. Are those displays multicultural, or does the majority culture predominate? What messages might those displays convey to students from minority groups?

RACE, CULTURE, AND ETHNICITY: ACTIVITY 5

Purpose

The purpose of this activity is to encourage school personnel to look beyond common cultural markers to the deep racial and ethnic values that shape each individual's view of the world.

Materials

- Book: I. Keido, *The Butterfly's Dream* (Boston: Tuttle, 2003). ISBN 0-8048-3480-6
- Flip chart
- Markers
- Overhead projector OR
- Computer projection screen on which you can itemize responses

Abstract of the Children's Book

The book is a collection of seven short stories based on the teachings of the great Zen master and Taoist philosopher, Chuang-Tzu. The stories begin and end with the ponderings of Chuang-Tzu, who isn't sure if he's a man dreaming that he is a butterfly, or if he is a butterfly dreaming that he is a man dreaming that he is a butterfly. All of the stories are connected by this central theme of paradox, of learning to see the world in ways other than black and white, good or bad. Many of the values professed in this book differ sharply from the typical American values of industry, assertiveness, and certainty.

Setting the Stage

Note: This activity has three distinct parts. Question 1 should be answered before the task of question 2 is assigned; question 2 should be completed before question 3 is posed.

1. Make a list of as many indicators or examples of multiculturalism that can be found in your school. You have two minutes.
2. Categorize your list, clustering likes with likes. (Distinct categories might include holiday celebrations, music styles, language, clothing styles, or art objects.)
3. Would you characterize the categories on your list as having deep or superficial cultural meaning?

Notes on Reading the Book

This selection comprises seven short stories that are loosely woven together. All seven stories should be read aloud. The best reader for this selection should be able to comfortably pronounce Chinese names, as well as read the stories slowly and convincingly, therefore allowing the subtle messages of the stories to emerge.

Discussion Questions

1. How many items do you have on your list?
2. What are some of your categories? What level of cultural meaning did you assign to this category? Why?
3. How many of you had a category for value-centered ideas, or ways of thinking about the world?
4. How many of you created a category for food items? Is food on almost everyone's list? Why?

5. How do the stories reflect cultural values that may differ from our own?

6. Were you perplexed by the meaning and relevance of these stories? Did you have trouble understanding them? Why or why not?

Facilitating the Discussion

1. Encourage a sharing of categories and lists, making note of the common items and categories that emerge. Post these categories on an overhead, computer projection screen, or a flip chart.

2. What categories have emerged? Did many of the participants have common lists?

3. Which of the categories that you've come up with are indicative of deep, versus superficial, values or meanings?

4. How did you decide which were which?

Note: Some of the educators who hear these stories may fail to understand their depth and meaning. This, sadly, is precisely the point: Many cultures that differ from ours not only have alternative ways of creating art, speaking, or working, but those cultures also interpret human behavior and intention differently than does the majority culture in America. Multiculturalism is really a different way of seeing, and making sense of, the world. Although as human beings we share many common needs, the manifestation of those needs, and the meaning we attach to our experiences, the values we judge as primary, and decrees about the best way to "be in the world" often differ markedly. Thus, for most of us, our experiences with multiculturalism center on concrete things like food or clothing styles. These stories are thus excellent exemplars of the power of multiculturalism at a deep, rather than superficial, level.

Other Metaphorical Uses or Parallels

This text could be used as a metaphor on the fragility of what we call reality, the limits of positivist thinking, or as an introduction to Eastern philosophies.

Illustrations

The chalk-and-pastel drawings by Kazuko Stone are based on drawings she made in China. The details on some pictures are quite small and may be hard to see if the book is simply held up before the session's participants.

Recommended Background Reading

I. Bruder, "Multicultural Education: Responding to the Demographics of Change," *Electronic Learning* 12, no. 2 (1992): 20–26; G. Feng and J. English, *Chuang Tsu: Inner Chapters* (New York: Vintage, 1974); C. Thorp, "Web Wonders/Equity and Opportunity," *Educational Leadership* 60, no. 4 (2002–2003): 96.

Insight into Action

How well do we know our students, particularly those whose cultural, ethnic, or racial backgrounds differ from our own? What opportunities do we provide those students to share with the school community all of who they are? When and how are their parents welcomed into the fabric of school life? As you celebrate Women's History Month, Black History Month, and other holidays and events, make special efforts to garner input and ideas from diverse segments of the community. Invite guest speakers who can address the diversity of ideas and customs, and the meaning and values beneath them.

RACE, CULTURE, AND ETHNICITY: ACTIVITY 6

Purpose

The purpose of this activity is to learn more about the Middle Eastern cultures that have been part of the history that has shaped those individuals who come to the United States from that part of the world.

Materials

- Book: F. P. Heide and J. H. Gilliland, *The Day of Ahmed's Secret* (New York: Lothrop, Lee & Shepard, 1990). ISBN 0-688-14023-8

Abstract of the Children's Book

This beautiful book tells the story of a boy growing up in Cairo who works hard to help his family amid the cacophony of city sounds and sights. He is proud of the strength he has developed to help his father in his work and shares two valuable lessons he learns. One lesson from his father is the value of growing strong, but not growing old. The other is his secret: he learns to write his name, which he views as placing him forever in history.

Setting the Stage

1. Think of a personal accomplishment that you have achieved and how you shared it with others.
2. Think of something one of your students has shared that she or he perceived as a major personal accomplishment. Why do you think she or he found it important to share?

Notes on Reading the Book

The book is a beautiful story of a boy who realizes his personal value and contributions to his family and community. The book should be read with a voice that honors that value. At the end, the wonder of his "secret" is that he can write his name. Read this with the awe of a young child who reveals his greatest talent.

Discussion Questions

1. Is Ahmed any different from any other child who has accomplished a major feat in his or her life? Why is writing his name so important?
2. Do the reasons for public schooling in the United States transcend the cultural, racial, and ethnic heritage of each student and teacher? How? Why?
3. Identify one or two things that you learned from the story about life in Cairo. Do you think it is like that now, or is this an old story? Support your perceptions.

Facilitating the Discussion

1. Clearly it is important here to help participants discuss the similarities among children when they discover a new skill or acquire new information. It is not bound by race, culture, or ethnicity.
2. Help teachers think through the role of public schooling in your community, your state, and in the United States generally. The historic role, of course, is education for an informed citizenry in a democracy. Have we lost sight of that? How can we ensure it?
3. Here you would expect teachers to discuss whether young children today are still working in places like Cairo (the answer is yes). Families who immigrate to this country are often unsure about our educational system and the impact on their lives from such a different system. Help teachers think about ways that they can learn more about the ethnic diversity in our communities.

Other Metaphorical Uses or Parallels

This book can be used to discuss the value of hard work and expectations for contributions from self to others, or the importance of family and traditions.

Illustrations

The illustrations are beautifully graphic of the city and its many sights. Ahmed is clearly depicted as a child who is working hard, but also keenly alert to things in his environment. Be sure to share the last several pages where he stands before his parents and displays his writing.

Recommended Background Reading

Race, culture, and ethnicity in education are covered extensively in the Harvard University Fellows program on the same topic. Available at www.gse.harvard.edu/news/features/postdoc09012001.html.

Insight into Action

Start a discussion group on ways that teachers can become better informed about the individual differences among the various ethnic, cultural, and racial groups that make up our communities. They might read articles, invite guest speakers (such as a parent from a given group who could address her desires for learning for her child), or visit the activities in the community that are sponsored by various ethnic societies, community organizations, or religious groups.

RACE, CULTURE, AND ETHNICITY: ACTIVITY 7

Purpose

The purpose of this activity is to consider what is known among faculty about students of Hispanic, or Latin, cultures.

Materials

- Book: P. D. Eastman, *Are You My Mother? ¿Eres tu mi mama?* (New York: Random House, 1988). ISBN 0-394-91596-8

Abstract of the Children's Book

This book is written in Spanish and English. The book is a classic children's story of a little bird trying to find his mother after she has gone to look for food. It illustrates the confusion the bird experiences when he doesn't have any basis for judging another "his mother."

Setting the Stage

1. Are there times when you feel confused or conflicted about the differences in your values and experiences and those of others with whom you come in contact?
2. Do you find yourself trying to avoid such contacts, or do you look for ways that you can connect?

Notes on Reading the Book

If possible, have two readers for the book reading in English and Spanish simultaneously, or read one passage in English and then the next in Spanish. (Another way to read is to divide the group randomly in two groups

and have one hear the story in Spanish and one in English.) The importance
of reading the book in both languages is to show that in spite of language
differences there is a shared norm of what is important and what is valued.

Discussion Questions

1. If you had heard the book in Spanish only, would you have thought
   about the similarities of the hunt for identity that the little bird experienced when he asked all the different animals and the power
   digger? Why? Why not?
2. List three ways that you honor the cultural, ethnic, or racial differences among your students.
3. What are the dangers in assuming that students who share a race
   (e.g., Hispanic) also share a culture? How can/do you address this
   in your classes?

Facilitating the Discussion

1. For those teachers who do not speak Spanish, it is important to
   help them identify their frustration in not hearing the story in English. They could not make sense of it without the English translation. Talk about how this relates to feelings students have when
   they can't understand a concept (even in the same language) or the
   language of instruction.
2. Ask teachers to write their individual responses and then collect
   those to share via a newsletter or online listserv or website.
3. Just because students have a racial similarity does not mean they
   have a cultural similarity. For example, students from Mexico have
   different cultural experiences than students from Guatemala or
   Venezuela. It is important to help teachers think about their own
   preconceived ideas about these similarities. Help them identify
   ways that they can incorporate their students' ethnic, cultural, or
   racial identity into their lessons through sharing.

Other Metaphorical Uses or Parallels

This book can also be used to talk about family connections and feelings of loss when family structures change.

Illustrations

The simplistic illustrations show the effort on the part of the mother bird to provide for her child, and the child's curiosity and concern for finding his mother.

Recommended Background Reading

Race, culture, and ethnicity in education are covered extensively in the Harvard University Fellows program on the same topic. Available at www.gse.harvard.edu/news/features/postdoc09012001.html.

Insight into Action

From discussion question 2, share the ideas that are generated to identify curricular ways that teachers honor and celebrate the ethnic, racial, or cultural heritage that students bring to the class.

GENDER: ACTIVITY 1

Purpose

The purpose of this activity is to help school personnel identify the conscious (and unconscious) societal barriers that restrict boys from achieving their full intellectual, creative, and emotional potential, as well as to recognize the paradoxical messages that are sent to men in our society. The focus of this exercise is geared specifically around the experiences of African American adolescents and boys about what is valued and expected of them, and how those expectations may hinder, rather than nurture, their development.

Materials

- Book: T. Feelings, *Soul Looks Back in Wonder* (New York: Dial, 1993). ISBN 0-8037-1001-1

Note: From this book, use the following poems: Eugene Redmond, "boyz n search of their soular system," Mwatabu Okantah, "window morning," Haki R. Madhubuti, "Destiny," and Langston Hughes, "To You."

Copies of Setting the Stage questions need to be distributed to each of *six* groups as follows: if you have thirty people, you will need five copies of each question and will distribute question 1 to each member of group 1, question 2 to each member of group 2, and so on.

Abstract of the Children's Book

With artwork based on drawings done in Ghana and Senegal, West Africa, by Tom Feelings, this book is a collection of poems by thirteen African American poets, including Maya Angelou, Margaret Walker, and Alexis De Veaux. The poems are united by their celebration of the ancestry, creativity, and struggles of people of African origin; the illustrations by Feelings speak volumes.

Setting the Stage

1. Ask the group to count off in sixes. Then ask all of the ones to meet together, the twos to meet together, and so on. Announce to the large group, "You have three minutes to complete the task I'll give you. Work together in your group without telling members of other groups your specific task."
2. Give the following assignments to each group, in writing:

Group 1: Make a list of behaviors of the "typical boy" (if school is an elementary school) or the "typical male adolescent" (if at a middle, junior, or senior high school).

Group 2: Make a list of behaviors exhibited by people who are emotionally healthy.

Group 3: Make a list of behaviors that society (in general) considers taboo for boys and male adolescents.

Group 4: Given societal norms, make a list of five careers that are deemed most suitable for men.

Group 5: Given societal norms, make a list of five careers that are deemed unsuitable or questionable for men.

Group 6: List as many famous African American men that you can. ("Famous" means they have instantaneous name recognition in American culture.)

Notes on Reading the Book

Given the focus of this activity, an African American male is the best choice to read this book. The ideal reader has the ability to capture the lyrical cadence of the poems in this book, as well as expressing the emotive power of the selections.

Discussion Questions

There is no handout for the discussion.

1. For Group 6: Ask a group spokesperson to read the task, and the group's response to the assignment. ("List as many famous African American men as you can, with 'famous' defined as instantaneous name recognition in American culture.") Total up the names. After the group reads the list, ask, "What does this list say about who and what are valued in American society? Specifically, how many names are those of athletes or entertainers? How many names are left when those names are crossed off? What does the list say about behaviors of African American men that are recognized and valued? For Groups 1, 2, and 3: Ask a representative of each group to come forward. Ask them to share their task and the group's response to that task. Do you notice any contradictions between the lists? For example, are some of the behaviors noted as "exhibited by people who are emotionally healthy" the same type of behaviors that are viewed as taboo? What messages are we sending to male students? Are we questioning or reinforcing these mixed messages?

2. For Groups 4 and 5: Ask a representative to come forward to share their assignments and their lists. What values are implicit in these lists? How do these lists conform to or contradict the other group's ideas? What do your lists say about the power of the dominant culture to shape notions of what type of "life's work" is acceptable and valuable?

Facilitating the Discussion

1. There are no right or wrong answers to this activity, and it is important that the person who facilitates the discussion focus on the interaction among the group members as they struggled to compose

their lists. The facilitator should probe for agreement and dissent among the group members, for the messages we send to young boys are contradictory and confusing. It is likely that these "mixed messages" will be reflected in individual contributions to the small group discussion.

2. The large group discussion may pivot around humor, anger, or incredulity. It is important that the facilitator be comfortable managing the emotions that may emerge, as well as keeping the group on task.

3. At the close of the activity, the facilitator may choose to read Tom Feelings's introduction to the book, as it places the poems in a larger social context.

Other Metaphorical Uses or Parallels

This book could be used to facilitate a discussion of the African American experience in America, multiculturalism, Afrocentrism, self-esteem, or creativity.

Illustrations

This text may be valued for its powerful artwork as well as its text. Feelings's illustrations were constructed using sepia paper, colored pencils, and various types of papers to create collages. The book was a Book-of-the-Month Club selection; it was most probably selected for its powerful images as well as amazing words.

Recommended Background Reading

J. Canada, "Raising Better Boys," *Educational Leadership* 59, no. 6 (2000): 14–17.

Insight into Action

The follow-up to this activity is to design an activity to help boys and young men in schools confront the emotional and social straight jackets that are imposed on them. One avenue to explore is the use of African American mentors who can visit the school, interact with students, and model a different way of "being" in the world. If your school doesn't currently have a mentoring program for boys, why not? In order to establish or reinvigorate a program, what needs to be done? African American churches may be willing allies, as are local men's organizations. Do not assume it can't be done. Many men are just waiting to be asked. For resources and suggestions, see examples at this website: www.sacnas.org/k12.html.

GENDER: ACTIVITY 2

Purpose

The purpose of this activity is to explore the stereotypes related to gender, in this case, those specific to females and what teachers can do to address them.

Materials

- Book: R. N. Munsch, *The Paperbag Princess* (Ontario: Annick, 1985). ISBN 0-920-236162

Abstract of the Children's Book

The main character in the book lives the life of a princess until the dragon comes along and burns down her castle and steals her prince. She uses cunning and bravery (even though she has to resort to a paper bag dress, as it is the only thing not burned up) to free her prince. In the end she walks away after rescuing him because he is more concerned about what she is wearing than the fact that she was able to use her brain to free him.

Setting the Stage

1. Are there certain characteristics or behaviors that you identify as being specifically male or female? For example, "women wear makeup." Write down two or three for each gender.

2. Have you ever felt limited by others in something you wanted to do because you received feedback that suggested it was not appropriate for you? For example, "Men don't cry."

Notes on Reading the Book

The book will be best read by a woman who can express the demure voice of a princess who is protected, the developing voice of a young woman who uses her brain to solve a problem against the dragon, and the mature voice of a young woman who refuses to be connected with someone who limits her because of her appearance.

Discussion Questions

1. In what ways was the princess able to outwit the dragon?
2. Was the princess offended by the response of the prince who focused only on her appearance and not her ability to free him? What evidence do you have for that?
3. What kinds of phrases can teachers use that will not limit student progress or interests based on their gender?

Facilitating the Discussion

1. The princess challenged the dragon by appealing to his vanity about his abilities and got him to exhaust his strength.
2. The princess appeared to be offended when the prince focused on how she was dressed. The evidence is in her unwillingness to continue a relationship with him, thus negating the "happily ever after" fairy tale.
3. Get teachers to talk about gender neutral language. For example, what is the difference in talking about a *postal carrier* versus a *postman*?

Other Metaphorical Uses or Parallels

This book can also be used to discuss problem solving strategies. Another use of this book is to examine the role of the prince and why he felt it was necessary to focus on the princess' attire rather than her ability to rescue him.

Illustrations

The illustrations are pastels that show the princess changing from her protected role in the castle to a problem solver. As she manages to outwit the dragon, the illustrations show her becoming more confident, then her realization that the prince was not interested in her as a person, but in her appearance.

Recommended Background Reading

M. Piper, *And Jill Came Tumbling After* (Morristown, FL: Ritamelia, 1996).

Insight into Action

Have teachers pair/share to practice some of their phrases that do not limit the views that students have of what they can do based on gender. Ask them to identify and share any particularly good responses so that the whole group can hear them.

GENDER: ACTIVITY 3

Purpose

The purpose of this activity is to discuss the ways that teachers can help change the limitations that we place on children and young people when we arbitrarily define what they can accomplish based on gender.

Materials

- Book: A. Johnson, *Just Like Josh Gibson* (New York: Simon & Schuster Books for Young Readers, 2004). ISBN 0-689-82628-1

Abstract of the Children's Book

This wonderful book tells the simple story of a little girl who was taught to play baseball by her father and had to watch from the sidelines while the boys got to play in the league games. It was her dream to be "just like Josh Gibson" and she did not see herself limited by being a girl. She had the opportunity once as a young girl to feel the exhilaration of playing the game well (when a boy was too hurt to play) but never had the opportunity to pursue her desire to play baseball with "the boys."

Setting the Stage

1. Think about your childhood. Identify three activities that were clearly limited by the gender of the individuals participating.
2. Even if you never wanted to pursue an activity generally limited to those of the opposite sex, do you know someone who would like to have had the opportunity to do something generally limited to one gender or the other? What was it?

Notes on Reading the Book

Read the book several times, since there are not many words in it, and become so familiar with it that you can tell it more than read it. This story begs to be shared as a story being passed from one generation to another, with the reality that some things have not changed much. If the book is read by a woman (particularly one of African American heritage), it can be very powerful.

Discussion Questions

1. Did Grandmama educate or embitter her granddaughter by sharing the story of her own experience in playing baseball?
2. Even if you personally think that some activities or professions should be gender specific, as a public educator do you attempt to ensure that you do not limit the appeal or opportunity of a

profession or activity to individuals based on gender? Do you think about how your behavior can influence children and young people?

3. List activities in school that include individuals, regardless of gender, and those that are gender exclusive. Identify one that is gender exclusive for males and one that is gender exclusive for females.

Facilitating the Discussion

1. Emphasize that Grandmama was both sharing her history to inform her granddaughter about a sport that she valued and treasured and, at the same time, was planting a seed for her to consider the limitations of defining others by sex, race, or class.

2. Teachers should be able to state that they (1) are objective in presenting the pros and cons of activities or professions, (2) encourage children and young people to look for examples of people who have been nontraditional in their pursuits (e.g., Madam Curie, Christa MacAuliffe, a male nurse) when they discuss the opportunities open to them from successful pursuit of their dreams (whether academic, the arts, or athletics).

3. Ask the participants to list the activities for themselves first and then share them with the group. List them on a board or chart paper. Once they have been identified, discuss ways that these activities can be strengthened by creating opportunities for the opposite gender to be actively involved (e.g., women as football trainers, sports announcers, etc.).

Other Metaphorical Uses or Parallels

This book provides a wonderful vehicle for looking at the importance of history on who we are as individuals in a family and community. It can also provoke a discussion about why it was okay for the young girl to play when someone was hurt and they needed another player, but not to play on a routine basis. How often does perceived necessity affect our willingness to "overlook" the boundaries that have been placed on sports, careers, and life activities in general?

Illustrations

Beautiful soft colors in strong poignant drawings bring this story to life. It is easy to see the femininity that was expected and maintained for Grandmama even when she was playing baseball by the illustrations of her dresses and hair bows. But, the role of her father in teaching her to play the game and the community to "inviting her in" when she was needed gave her hope that she could have a positive effect on changing others' beliefs (see her face when she starts the story with her grand-daughter) in limiting an individual based on irrelevant factors that were clearly unwarranted.

Recommended Background Reading

American Psychological Association, "Cartoons Still Stereotype Gender Roles," APA news release, 1997. See also works by Alice Kessler-Harris on women's labor.

Insight into Action

Consider doing a serious evaluation of the programs and activities in your school that could be more gender neutral (i.e., "rules" that exclude students from organizations based on gender). Help teachers understand that this discussion is not about eliminating activities that have more appeal to one gender than another, but to recognize that our behaviors as educators can have a profound effect on children and young people in limiting their vision for themselves when we define things by gender, race, socioeconomic level, and so on. Can anyone remember when Little League was exclusively for boys?

4

COMMUNITY CONUNDRUMS

OVERVIEW AND BACKGROUND

In an increasingly complex, confusing world that has instantaneous communication, it is no wonder that many aspects of life in the twenty-first century emerge as conundrums. Merriam-Webster's online dictionary defines a conundrum as "an intricate and difficult problem." The community conundrums that have an effect on the schooling of students in the United States are many and often defy our ability to grasp, much less address. The topics chosen for this chapter are the result of many discussions with educators who expressed concerns about the effects on their students of issues related to these topics. While it is understood that other conundrums exist in different communities, it is hoped that the dialogue begun through these topics will lead to others that can be beneficial to serving the students in a particular school or community. The topics in this chapter are family structures, family norms and school expectations, culture of violence, health issues, peer pressure, equality and fairness, effects of media, and economic uncertainties.

Often assumptions are made that students in our schools live in what is generally called the traditional family—two parents with their biological children. Yet, more and more teachers know that many of their students do not live in that traditional family and realize that the performance of their students is often affected by the family structure in which they live. Some students live in two-parent households with their biological parents and biological siblings. Many others live in two-parent families but are not biologically related to one or both of the parents, or one or more of their siblings. Other students live with a single parent, in foster homes, or with grandparents or other relatives. Sometimes these family compositions are due to death or the necessity that children be raised by someone other than the birthparents. What is important in the discussion to be held under this topic is for educators to examine their own beliefs, and sometimes their own prejudices, about what constitutes a family. The activities will provide an opportunity for looking at different family structures and the needs of children and young people regardless of who is raising them.

Closely following the need to discuss family structures is the need to examine family norms and school expectations. These are often very similar based on the community in which a school resides. However, there are times when the situation in a family precludes the kind of involvement that teachers would like to see for students. The activities that are provided in this topic are based on the importance of considering the expectations of a given school community. Additionally, discussions need to occur on ways teachers can help students be successful, even if the family situation cannot support the importance of education and norms expressed at school.

The culture of violence activities are designed to help educators consider the effects of violence on students in their day-to-day world. In some communities, violence is a part of daily life. In other communities violence is not witnessed by many students other than their exposure to the media to which they are exposed or the games that are part of their activities. Whatever the exposure to violence, there is no doubt that many educators are concerned about the increasingly violent responses that some students exhibit in the school environment. The activities under this topic provide educators with the chance to discuss and examine their own communities and expectations and ways that they can reduce the effects of a violence-saturated culture.

In the world of 1950s television, no one got sick, communicable dis-
eases were under control, and cures to dreaded illnesses were found.
But in the reality of the twenty-first century, no one is untouched by the
effects of health issues, whether directly or indirectly. Even for those
with access to the most sophisticated medical care, our health challenges have an effect on schools and the teachers and students. Whether
the health issue is a parent who is sick, a student who has a major disease, or a beloved member of the school community who is ill, there is
no escaping the effects that health can have on the educational process.
Often educators do not even consider this topic until someone in their
school is affected. Yet, the opportunity to talk about the issues of health
and how students and faculty are affected can better prepare educators
to face such issues when they arise. The activities in this section provide
a cross-section of health topics for discussion.

As hard as parents and teachers try to educate and teach values and
behavioral norms in a group, peer pressure continues to concern parents and educators alike. Typically peer pressure has been viewed as a
negative effect on the actions of children and young people. Often such
concerns as smoking and alcohol consumption are assumed to begin by
peer pressure. Clearly parents and teachers see children and young
people influenced by what their peers wear and do. There are, however, positive outcomes from peer pressure. School communities where
students support each other to behave appropriately, and to be successful and contributing members of their communities, are several examples of positive peer pressure. Educators have the opportunity to
consider both positive and negative peer pressure through discussions
and activities that allow them to examine their own beliefs about peer
pressure and to consider ways that they can use peer pressure for the
good of their students.

Equality and fairness are often topics that arise in schools among
educators and the community members they serve. Although the U.S.
Constitution clearly states that all men are created equal, most educators know that treating every student equally is rarely possible. However, it is possible to treat all students fairly. Students often question
issues of equality and fairness, and without the opportunity for educators to discuss what they believe, it is unlikely that students will see

consistency among those who teach them. Activities under this topic provide examples for discussion that help educators clarify issues of equality and fairness.

If one questions even a small number of educators about the effects of media on students today, the responses will likely indicate that teachers believe that the media has a major effect on student beliefs, thoughts, and actions. With the speed of information transmission via cell phones, hand held computers with wireless connections, television, and the movies, it is unlikely that the more traditional schooling environment where student knowledge was highly dependent on teacher lectures and textbooks can survive for much longer. Yet helping educators use the technologies to the advantage of student learning and considering both the positive and negative effects of the speed and quantity of information available will require much consideration and discussion. Participation in the activities under this topic will provide educators a starting point for examining their own classrooms and their schools and how media affects their students.

Last, but certainly not least, one of the biggest conundrums in the United States today is economic uncertainty. There was a time when for most adults in our society, economic status was reasonably stable, but the last decade has clearly changed the perception that most adults have about the stability of employment, the security of retirement funds, and the ability to provide for themselves and their families. These concerns have dramatic effects on both children and adults in our society. Issues such as homelessness, minimal resources, and access to goods and services are but a few of the ideas that can be explored in this topic.

In all of these intricate and difficult problems, yes, there are conundrums. With considered dialogue and serious commitment to take the concept of Insight into Action provided in each of the activities, educators have the opportunity to improve the world in which their students live and help them find solutions for their personal futures and the future of our nation. As Christa McAuliffe, the first educator-astronaut, said, "I touch the future. I teach." Addressing these conundrums will strengthen the contributions that educators make to their communities through the education of children and young people.

TOPICS AND BOOKS DISCUSSED IN CHAPTER 4

Family structures, 162–73
  Love You Like Crazy Cakes
  Singing with Momma Lou
  Little Duck Lost
  Let's Talk about It: Adoption
Family norms and school expectations, 173–81
  Moonthief
  The Remarkable Farkle McBride
  Many Moons
Culture of violence, 181–88
  Smoky Night
  Mr. Lincoln's Way
  The Missing Piece Meets the Big O
Health issues, 189–97
  Our Mom Has Cancer
  Doctor De Soto
  Princess Alopecia
Peer Pressure, 197–205
  Finklehopper Frog
  Chrysanthemum
  Hilda Must Be Dancing
Equality and fairness, 205–13
  Tops and Bottoms
  Tar Beach
  Sometimes Bad Things Happen
The effects of media, 213–22
  Librarian from the Black Lagoon
  Mole Music
  The True Story of the Three Little Pigs
  Salt in His Shoes
Economic uncertainties, 222–36
  Fairytale News
  The Fish's Tale
  Uptown

Peppe the Lamplighter
The Salamander Room

FAMILY STRUCTURES: ACTIVITY I

Purpose

The purpose of this activity is to help teachers understand the contradictory and paradoxical values that undergird what we call family values and to explore the common experiences of children's familial experiences, whether the family is formed by second marriages and stepchildren, by first marriage and biological children, by single parenthood, by adoption, or by gay or lesbian commitments.

Materials

- Book: R. Lewis, *I Love You Like Crazy Cakes* (Boston: Little, Brown, 2000). ISBN: 0-316-52538-3. Note: The facilitator must be comfortable leading a discussion that touches on racism, homophobia, and deeply held personal values regarding the meaning of family.

Abstract of the Children's Book

An adoptive mother tells the story of her quest to adopt her Chinese daughter, the poignancy of their first meeting, the beginning of their relationship, and their joint journey to America to begin their lives together as a new family.

Setting the Stage

Instruct participants that no one will see their answers to the following questions:

1. Quickly jot down your first thoughts when you hear the phrase "single mother."

2. Quickly jot down your first thoughts when you hear the phrase "traditional family."
3. Quickly jot down your first thoughts when you hear the phrase "multiracial family."
4. Quickly jot down your first thoughts when you hear the phrase "blended family."

Notes on Reading the Book

This book should be read by a woman who is able to convey great affection in her voice, as the narrator is "talking" to her daughter.

Discussion Questions

1. Would your sentiments regarding this story be different if the author was a divorced woman with other children?
2. Would your sentiments regarding this story be different if the author was a lesbian?

Facilitating the Discussion

1. Without revealing your responses to the questions from the Setting the Stage activity, from where or from whom did you acquire your perspective on a traditional family? Multiracial family? Single-parent family? Blended family?
2. Do we tend to look at the situation described in this book differently than we view other single mothers? Why or why not?
3. The book ends with the phrase "safe and happy in the world." What assumptions do we make about what conditions equate to "safe and happy"? How does that assumption limit our perspective on family structures or subcultures different from our own?
4. How do we as teachers honor and respect children's home experiences?

Other Metaphorical Uses or Parallels

Although it is a subtext in this book, the issues of pain and loss are ever present. Similarly, this book could be used to provoke discussions of the status of children worldwide, particularly orphans in developing countries, the human rights situation of children, and the meaning of motherhood.

Illustrations

Jane Dyer's large watercolor illustrations capture the fragility and beauty of this family's beginnings. Pay special attention to the inside of the orphanage; the typical orphanage looks nothing like that.

Recommended Background Reading

Lambda Legal Fund (www.lambdalegal.org); Parents without Partners (www.parentswithoutpartners.org).

Insight into Action

Take an inventory of classroom practices and discussions. Are students' feelings regarding their family validated by classroom texts, displays, and discussions? Are beginning teachers prepared for the types and variety of family circumstances that are common and uncommon in your community? Does your school–community relations plan include efforts to involve parents and guardians from diverse family structures? Are concrete efforts made to meet the special needs of these families? Are professionals in your school caring and communicative and all employees sensitive to and respectful of diverse family constellations? As Adrienne Rich wrote, "When someone with the authority of, say, a teacher, describes the world and you are not in it, there is a sense of disequilibrium, as if you looked into a mirror and saw nothing."

Author's note: As a mother of a child of a different race from her parents, I, Julie, can speak with some authority about the seemingly benign questions and comments that, while innocent on the surface, can be deeply disturbing to a child and/or parent. Although a family situation may seem "strange" to school personnel, to the child, that same situation is perfectly normal; it's home.

And sadly, for too many children, the phrase "there's no place like home" really means, "There's no place like home, no matter how bad it is."

As Jacque always says, "Children do not choose the circumstances into which they are born, nor in which they live; we must teach each one."

FAMILY STRUCTURES: ACTIVITY 2

Purpose

The purpose of this activity is for the participants to discuss the needs of students who are dealing with the effects on the family of aging parents or grandparents.

Materials

- Book: L. J. Altman, *Singing with Momma Lou* (New York: Lee & Low, 2002). ISBN 1-58430-040-X

Abstract of the Children's Book

This lovely children's book tells the story of a young girl whose grandmother is suffering from Alzheimer's disease. Although her parents take her to visit her grandmother in a nursing home, she is not sure what to do or say. As she begins to learn things that her grandmother used to do, she sets about bringing together memorabilia of her grandmother's participation in civil rights marches and her beautiful ability to sing. In addition to being able to share them with her grandmother, she learns that she has a beautiful heritage steeped in her grandmother's memories leaves.

Setting the Stage

1. Have you had a family member or friend who has (or had) Alzheimer's disease or dementia? What are the main things you think about with those conditions?
2. How do you think the loss of memory of a loved one affects the students you teach? Are you aware of any who are currently going through this life event?

Notes on Reading the Book

Select a reader who can reflect the childish innocence that Tamika brings to the story as she tries to relate to her grandmother and make a connection through her grandmother's memorabilia.

Discussion Questions

1. As more students and their families are affected by an aging baby boom population, what do you think will be the effects on the family by those affected by Alzheimer's or dementia?
2. What is the message in this book that can be shared about the power of connections?
3. What service-learning activities do we have in our school to help children and young people to become better informed about the needs of the elderly in our community?

Facilitating the Discussion

1. More parents of today's students will find their time taken with the needs of aging parents (baby boom generation) and the attendant illnesses such as Alzheimer's and dementia. Help the participants to think about ways that they can identify the impact of this in their community.
2. As in all discussions of family structures, the power of connections to our history and/or roots is powerful. People generally want to know how their families influence them. The discussion of biological, as well as blended or adopted, families and how each contributes to who we are is evident when we consider Tamika's growing understanding about her grandmother's life.
3. Prior to the discussion, identify whatever information you have available about the service learning projects in your school. If you are not currently doing service learning projects, look for projects that will help you discuss this idea with faculty as a way of engaging students in their community and considering their curriculum in the context of their community.

Other Metaphorical Uses or Parallels

This book could also be used to discuss faculty work life, which is a topic in the second volume of this series.

Illustrations

The illustrations in this book are described in the *School Library Journal* as "expressive acrylic paintings . . . rich in color and emotion." The beauty of the humanity portrayed through these illustrations will move participants to think beyond themselves to the needs of others.

Recommended Background Reading

Information is available from the Alzheimer Association website: www.alz.org; Alzheimer's Disease Education and Referral (ADEAR) Center website: www.alzheimers.org; Alzheimer's Disease Core Center (ADCC) website: www.brain.nwu.edu/core/index.htm.

Insight into Action

If your school does not currently have a service learning program, develop a group to look at ways that you could participate in such activities. These may be a schoolwide project or individual requirements depending on the age of the students. If you have a service learning program, look for ways that the activities in which students participate can be used in connection with areas of study across the curriculum.

FAMILY STRUCTURES: ACTIVITY 3

Purpose

The purpose of this activity is to help teachers examine the roles their students play in their respective families and how the structure of that family may prompt the child or young adult to have feelings of isolation or alienation.

Materials

- Book: E. Briers, *Little Duck Lost* (New York: Dutton Children's Books, 2003). ISBN 0-525-47232-0

Abstract of the Children's Book

A young duck is born and heads out in search of where he belongs. He encounters many animals along the way who are willing to give him directions or connect him with another animal that is believed to have the answer to where he belongs. In the end, the little duck is reunited with his mother and finds peace and joy in being connected to his family.

Setting the Stage

1. Think about one student you have had in class (or known) who was unsure of his or her place in the family in which she or he lived. What were some of the concerns of that student?
2. Even when a child or young person lives with both biological parents and biological siblings, is it possible for him or her to be unsure of how he fits into the family structure?

Notes on Reading the Book

A quick read of the book will provide a framework for understanding that even though he was lost, the duckling continued to search for his connection to his family. Inflections should represent the desire he has to belong and the lengths to which he is willing to go to find that connection.

Discussion Questions

1. Why do you think the duck never gave up trying to find his home?
2. How does his example differ from students who exhibit extreme behaviors in their efforts to belong? What are some of the extremes to which students go to belong, whether in their family structure or among their peers?

3. Do faculty suppress efforts by children and young people to search for their connections through rules and regulations that are generally designed to maintain a safe, orderly environment?

Facilitating the Discussion

1. Explore the possibility with participants that because the duckling started his journey early in his life, he had not had others to tell him he could *not* do something, thus limiting his expectations.
2. Discuss the relative compliance of the duck in following the direction of others on how to find where he belonged. Many students drift to fringe groups (e.g., gangs, extreme dress or hair) or participate in activities (e.g., drinking) as they know no other way to find a place to belong.
3. Place the participants in small groups to discuss their individual responses to this question and explore what school rules are necessary for the safety and well being of all and which have evolved over time and may need to be eliminated. For example, some schools still have rules about males wearing earrings (gender stereotype) when a safety rule about earrings might be about the length of the earring (so it doesn't catch on something and cause injury).

Other Metaphorical Uses or Parallels

This book can also be used to discuss relationships that are supportive of individual growth and development through exploration, inquiry, and security in knowing that someone (the mother duck) is "looking out for you."

Illustrations

Because there are raised images on the pages, it is important to pass the book around after reading it. There is a strong message in the elements that are depicted through this technique. The colors and accuracy in the gentle illustrations will bring images to the minds of participants as they consider the "lost ducklings" they have known as teachers.

Recommended Background Reading

National Parent Teacher Association website: www.pta.org.

Insight into Action

Based on the small group discussions in question 3, ask a committee to review the student handbook and faculty handbook to see if there are rules that limit students from the natural exploration that is a necessary part of developing self-identity. Create a discussion group, either on-line or through a book reading, that allows further exploration of the topic. A book like *The Pact*, by Davis, Hunt, and Jenkins (2003), which shows the positive power of peer support and developing personal identity in a family and community structure, can help teachers explore the needs of students raised in poverty, such as inner-city public housing.

FAMILY STRUCTURES: ACTIVITY 4

Purpose

The purpose of this activity is to help teachers think about how they address family structures. Educators often make comments based on their personal experience or values without consideration for different family structures.

Materials

- Book: F. Rogers, *Let's Talk about It: Adoption* (New York: Putnam & Grosset, 1998). ISBN 0-698-11625-9

Abstract of the Children's Book

This book provides a short narrative on what it means to be in a family, whether formed by birth or by adoption. It provides a glimpse of issues that are part of everyday life and addresses them as the reality for all families, regardless of how they are constituted. But it recognizes that a family is (or should be) about love.

Setting the Stage

1. When you think of the families of your students, what comes to mind in terms of who the students' parents or siblings are? How do you define family?

2. Can you identify at least one student you know who does not have a traditional family (one made up of two parents with their biological children)?

Notes on Reading the Book

The book is an easy read and should be read with the ease one feels when she or he knows love. A range of emotions are expressed, but they are connected to the security of family, no matter how the family members are related. Read through it once and you will be comfortable with sharing it.

Discussion Questions

1. What percentage of the students in class live in what is perceived as the traditional family (two parents with their biological children) in this country? Do you know? Do you assume that all children have two birth parents in the home?

2. What does this book share as the major and most important component of family?

3. What activities do we have in school that are based on "moms and dads" without thinking about who the parents for a student might be (e.g., father and daughter dances)?

Facilitating the Discussion

1. If possible, "guesstimate" the percentage of students in your school who live in the traditional American family. National statistics (Census 2000) show that approximately 67 percent of children under the age of eighteen in this country live with two parents, but not necessarily their birth parents. Approximately 28 percent live with either a mother only or father only. Approximately 5 percent live with neither parent but may live with a grandparent.

2. The book makes very clear that families are about people loving each other. One example that often helps teachers think about what this means for children came from a discussion by the author (Jacobs) with her mother-in-law, who questioned the ability of a child to be loved as much by a parent who was not genetically related. The author responded, "We live in a society that does not allow relatives to marry each other, yet we expect them to love, honor, and support each other. Why do we deny children the same opportunities to be loved, honored, and supported?" This idea may help others to think about the importance of relationships.

3. This discussion will vary depending on the grade levels encompassed in the discussion. Elementary teachers may need to consider such things as Mother's Day activities, Valentine's Day, and so on. Middle and High School teachers may need to think about how students are asked and/or encouraged to "bring a parent" to a given activity. The purpose of this is not to exclude anyone, but rather to consider ways to be inclusive. Some students live in homes with gay or lesbian parentage, and when the assumption is made that two parents are of different genders, the child may feel he cannot speak about his actual parents. Helping teachers use gender-neutral language is important. For example, a high school awards banquet that is designed to include family members may be phrased something like this: "Please invite any family member or support person you would like to have present to celebrate with you."

Other Metaphorical Uses or Parallels

This book may be used to talk about issues related to death, divorce, and loss.

Illustrations

The illustrations for this book are color photographs that are reflective of the cross-cultural family structures in the United States today. The pictures generally reflect male and female parents, but there are photographs with one parent (male or female) as well as mixed race families.

Recommended Background Reading

J. M. Fields and K. E. Smith, *Poverty, Family Structure, and Child Well-Being: Indicators from the SIPP* (Washington, D.C:. Population Division, U.S. Bureau of the Census, 1998). Available at www.census .gov/population/www/documentation/twps0023.html. *Children's Living Arrangements and Characteristics: March 2002* (Washington, D.C.: Census Bureau Report). Available at www.census.gov/prod/2003pubs/ p20-547.pdf.

Insight into Action

Discussion related to this particular book may lead to forming a book circle to discuss some of the popular books about adoptees and their families. This does not have to be a mandatory book reading but rather one that those who are interested in learning more about the topic could pursue.

FAMILY NORMS AND SCHOOL EXPECTATIONS: ACTIVITY I

Purpose

The purpose of this activity is to help teachers address ways to help students who experience conflict when they only know unacceptable ways (e.g., use of bad language or stealing things to give as gifts) to show the teacher or others in the school they care about them.

Materials

- Book: R. McGough, *Moonthief* (New York: Houghton Mifflin, 2002). ISBN 0-534-5481-5

Abstract of the Children's Book

This book shares the story of a bear, who, in trying to show his love for another bear, steals the moon. However, this causes confusion for the recipient. Betty, the receiving bear, makes clear at the end that what he stole should be returned and that all she cares about is him, not what he gives her.

Setting the Stage

1. Have you ever tried to share an idea with another person who did not understand what you were trying to say? Do you know why there was a misunderstanding?
2. Has anyone ever given you a gift that (1) was clearly beyond his or her economic means or (2) had obviously been used? What did you think?

Notes on Reading the Book

The book can be read as a tale of love, but for this activity, it should be read with an emphasis on Bobby's efforts to impress Betty or get attention from her. Likewise Betty's voice should become more and more dismayed as she realizes Bobby stole something (the moon) to get her attention. At the end, the reader's voice should reflect forgiveness and acceptance.

Discussion Questions

1. Did Bobby think about the effects of his actions in "stealing the moon" to get Betty's attention?
2. How were the conflicts in Bobby's views and Betty's views like the differences teachers and students sometimes have about right and wrong?
3. Are there conflicts of ideas or values in our school among students? Teachers? Administrators and teachers? Students and teachers? Administrators? How do they manifest themselves?

Facilitating the Discussion

1. Help participants focus on the fact that Bobby did not think about the consequences of his actions. This is true for all of us at times. Discuss his issues of acceptance, as an individual, while teaching

him to consider his actions and what happens when he fails to consider consequences.

2. Discuss adult reactions to student behavior. Do teachers see their jobs as teaching new behavior or do they exhibit intolerance for the behavior students bring to school? You might want to discuss the effects of teachers thinking that punishment teaches new behavior. While consequences must be appropriate for unacceptable behavior, teachers have an important role in teaching new behaviors.

3. Brainstorm examples of inappropriate behavior in your school. Start by asking each person to list one or two issues she or he sees. Then pair/share, list as a large group, and discuss, if time allows.

Other Metaphorical Uses or Parallels

This book can be used to point out the importance of two people interacting, even in a group.

Illustrations

The illustrations are bright and whimsical. You can point out Betty's stern expression when she tells him to return the moon. Point out Bobby's sadness when he realizes he disappointed her. Last, point out the importance of acceptance in the last illustration.

Recommended Background Reading

National Parent Teacher Association website: www.pta.org.

Insight into Action

Take the list generated in discussion question 3 and find commonalities. Then compose a plan to be brought back to the group to address the issues specific to your school. These might include training for teachers or programs/discussion for students (e.g., Character Counts).

FAMILY NORMS AND SCHOOL EXPECTATIONS: ACTIVITY 2

Purpose

The purpose of this activity is to explore the differences in family expectations and school expectations and how teachers might address them.

Materials

- Book: J. Lithgow, *The Remarkable Farkle McBride* (New York: Simon & Schuster Books for Young Readers, 2000). ISBN 0-689-83340-7

Abstract of the Children's Book

This book tells the story of a musical prodigy whose talent is indulged by his parents as they continue to support his interests in different instruments and their sounds. After many instruments are mastered and subsequently destroyed, Farkle finds his passion by directing all the instruments in the orchestra.

Setting the Stage

1. Have you dealt with a child, your own or one of your students, who showed varied interests in expression, whether musical, artistic, or athletic?
2. Do you think parents should make their child stick with a particular activity or talent (e.g., violin lessons) even when the child loses interest? Why? Why not?

Notes on Reading the Book

The language of this book is as lyrical as the instruments that Farkle learns to play. Read it with joy for the music he makes and disdain for the pain he experiences when he loses interest. Be sure to open up the last pages into the four page spread that shows how he was able to encompass all of his interests through directing.

Discussion Questions

1. Was Farkle different from students you have known who have shown a lack of interest in a particular activity, even when you know that they have talent?
2. If parents allow their child to pursue interests other than the early one for which they have shown some talent, are they "giving in" to the child?
3. In a system of education that values continuity, compliance, and completion, how can educators show flexibility to explore each student's interests and talents?

Facilitating the Discussion

1. Teachers should be able to give any number of examples of a student who has shown a particular talent (e.g., in mathematics) and has then moved on to something else and the parents have supported that transfer of interest. Get teachers to talk about their feelings relative to whether they felt frustration at what they perceived to be a lack of discipline to persist, or whether they were able to celebrate a child's diverse interests.
2. This particular question should evoke some feelings about what it takes to ensure that a child is learning the value of sticking to a task, but also learning that there are choices to be made regarding the development of talents and skills.
3. Have teachers write down three things that they do in class that represent "continuity," "compliance," and "completion." Then share these among the group. Ask each group to then think of one way that they could be flexible in "compliance," for example. If students are expected to sit down as soon as they enter the room, encouraging students to take a "different route" to their desks would be one example of flexibility in compliance. See how many teachers can come up with for each area and share them.

Other Metaphorical Uses or Parallels

This book can be used to explore the many creative activities that might satisfy an individual talent that a student has.

Illustrations

The illustrations are dramatic and colorful. The four-page spread at the end provides an unusual graphic representation of an orchestra and of the satisfaction Farkle experienced in finally learning that his talent is best used in directing.

Recommended Background Reading

Character education website: www.charactercounts.org.

Insight into Action

Plan a follow-up with teachers to discuss ways that they have been able to be flexible in the classroom and have addressed the ability of students to pursue different interests.

FAMILY NORMS AND SCHOOL EXPECTATIONS: ACTIVITY 3

Purpose

The purpose of this activity is to discuss the issues that students bring into the school environment—their hopes, their dreams, their beliefs— and how the various adults in the school environment may have different expectations from the student and from each other.

Materials

- Book: J. Thurber, *Many Moons* (Orlando, FL: Harcourt Brace, 1971). ISBN 0-15-251873-8. The book has been rereleased and is currently available.

Abstract of the Children's Book

This ageless tale of a parent's efforts to give his child all she desires is set in the fantasy world of a princess. In her father's efforts to gain the "moon" for her, he discovered, through his court jester, that the many different views offered by his advisers were right from their view of the world, but what really mattered was his daughter's view of what she wanted.

Setting the Stage

1. List three things you wanted as a child or adolescent that you received or achieved.
2. List three things you wanted as a child or adolescent that you did not receive or achieve.

Notes on Reading the Book

The book takes about five minutes to read. It is important to read it carefully before sharing it so that you can maintain momentum when reading the "list" of things that three of the characters recite to the king. This is important to ensure that each appears confident in his ability to assist the king, but at the same time is clearly unable to solve the problem the king presents. Read the words of the court jester with deference, but a lighthearted spirit that "nothing is beyond reach."

Discussion Questions

1. How were the wishes of Princess Lenore, while seemingly unrealistic, finally granted when someone took the time to find out how she perceived the moon?
2. In what ways do you see similarities between what Lenore wanted and her father wanted for her, and what students and parents want from teachers?
3. What are some ways that we, as teachers, can solve the differences between home and school (whether values, achievement goals, etc.) if we act like the court jester?

Facilitating the Discussion

1. After participants have had a couple of minutes to think for themselves of how Princess Lenore's wishes could be granted, call on

several people to provide their views. Emphasize those that include (or bring them out if not provided) (1) defining the components of the goal (e.g., size, shape), (2) understanding what she
wanted (e.g., gold), and (3) determining a way to address it (e.g.,
having the goldsmith make a necklace).

2. The king and princess reinforced each other's views and the
princess manipulated her father to get what she "thought" she
wanted (the moon). Students often manipulate parents to think
that teachers are unreasonable in their expectations, that somehow
the parent has to make things different, and teachers can be
caught in the middle.

3. Ask the participants to brainstorm ways that they can practice addressing conflicts in values or expectations so that there is support
among themselves and consistency for parents and students in
how issues are resolved. Discuss how sometimes the use of humor
and the willingness to accept that each person's view is "right"
from his or her perspective can assist in finding a compromise to
the problem.

Other Metaphorical Uses or Parallels

This book also provides the opportunity to look at the effects of organizational structures and/or bureaucratic controls and how teachers feel
with so many "experts" trying to solve the problems of our schools from
the outside.

Illustrations

The illustrations are beautiful pastel drawings that aptly reflect how
the father is trying to support his daughter's wishes and how the advisers are sure they are right, and have evidence to justify it, and the whimsical nature of dealing with wishes and reality through fantasy.

Recommended Background Reading

A. Levine, "It's a Sin to Deny Kids a Quality Education," *Curriculum
Review* 43, no. 4 (2003): 3–4.

Insight into Action

Follow up with teachers in a week to ten days after the discussion to assess ways they think they can support each other and provide a unified approach to problem solving when family values conflict with school expectations. Think of ways that the administration and faculty can work together to provide periodic checks to ensure that they are still in agreement on what and how they can and should address the conflicts that arise between home and school norms.

CULTURE OF VIOLENCE: ACTIVITY I

Purpose

The purpose of this activity is to explore the ways that teachers can help students who live in violent circumstances or through violent events to cope.

Materials

- Book: E. Bunting, *Smoky Night* (Orlando, FL: Harcourt Brace, 1994). ISBN 0-15-269954-6

Abstract of the Children's Book

This book tells the story of a young boy and his mother during the riots in Los Angeles. The emotions that the boy experiences in watching other people riot and loot and their expressions of anger and apparent "joy" are presented. Additionally, when the rioting results in arson of their apartment building, the boy has to deal with the potential loss of his cat and the emotions of living in a shelter with hostile or indifferent neighbors. The end result is the coming together of people who have experienced the unkindness of others.

Setting the Stage

1. Think about a time when you felt strong emotions as the result of extreme violence. It may be a personal event or the extended effects

of an event such as the 9/11 attacks. How did you feel? What emotions did you experience?

2. Can you identify one or more students who have struggled with violent events in their lives? What were their emotions? What were the effects on their ability to focus at school?

Notes on Reading the Book

The book is a short narrative on the reaction and emotions of rioters and those affected by it. Be sure to show the concern of the little boy in your voice when reading about the observations from a darkened room (use a hushed voice) and the fear (show anxiety in your voice) that his cat is lost. Show compassion in your voice when the people in the shelter begin to see how they can and should come together in their community and support each other.

Discussion Questions

1. What emotions did you hear in the boy as a result of the events he witnessed? Do you think they are the emotions that most people would experience in the circumstances?
2. How is school environment affected by widely publicized social unrest, such as the Los Angeles riots? Is school a safe place for students and teachers?
3. What things do teachers do to show that it is possible to resolve differences, to be a community, and to accept different points of view?

Facilitating the Discussion

1. Elicit comments that reflect the curiosity about why the looters looked happy, why they expressed anger, and the fear that the boy had in the fire. It is important here to help the participants consider that many emotions are evoked in situations such as this.
2. Data on the number of referrals for discipline in your school can prove very helpful to focus participants on the relative "safe" environment of your school. Sometimes teachers do not see the anger

that is expressed by some students because they are only aware of the students with whom they deal. Having data that show the number of referrals for aggressive actions, for example, and the number of repeat offenders, can help to determine what needs to be done to help students find better ways of resolving differences.

3. Ask teachers to think about disagreements that they have had with each other or challenges to other ideas and how they resolved them. Do they "agree to disagree" if they cannot reach common ground? Do they encourage students to participate in active debates on issues in order to hear more than one point of view? Record these responses to share.

Other Metaphorical Uses or Parallels

This book can also be used to talk about family norms and school expectations.

Illustrations

The illustrations are multidimensional because the illustrator used paper to create depth and express the confusion one experiences in difficult situations. The use of everyday items such as clothes hangers provides a strong reality-based visual.

Recommended Background Reading

S. M. Crow and S. J. Hartman, "Responding to Threats of Workplace Violence: The Effects of Culture and Moral Panic," *Health Care Manager* 22, no. 4 (2003): 340–49.

Insight into Action

From discussion question 3, think of ways that the faculty and staff can model ways of resolving differences which create an environment where different views are valued and accepted. This might evolve from a reading group that focuses on ideas from schools that have had to deal with violent situations.

CULTURE OF VIOLENCE: ACTIVITY 2

Purpose

The purpose of this activity is to share the importance of educators' roles in the lives of children and young people who may need someone to intervene in a cycle of violence.

Materials

- Book: P. Polacco, *Mr. Lincoln's Way* (New York: Philomel, 2001). ISBN 0-399-23754-2

Abstract of the Children's Book

This book is the story of a principal, a really cool principal, who is challenged by the needs of a young man who expresses anger and cruelty toward others. Mr. Lincoln finds a way to actively engage the student in responsibilities around the school and encourages him to become a positive member of the community.

Setting the Stage

1. Think of one student you have helped in your career to see the world in a more positive light than she or he did prior to your intervention.
2. What kinds of things did you do to engage this young person and move him or her from a negative perspective?

Notes on Reading the Book

This book is best read by a male voice, so if you are not male, invite someone on your staff (or a guest) to read it. This will give more power to the voice of the principal and the little boy. A read through will show how the principal can be firm, caring, and strong and lead a young man who needs direction. Be sure to read the last two sentences in which Eugene's future is revealed.

Discussion Questions

1. How is the role of Mr. Lincoln pivotal in Eugene's development?
2. What are some of the things that you can do to help students find the best in themselves and develop it?
3. What are some ways that a faculty can share the positive growth in humane values exhibited by students?

Facilitating the Discussion

1. Elicit responses from participants and focus on the idea that as an educational leader Mr. Lincoln did not just deal with the effects of the student's behavior, but he saw his responsibility as an educator to help him find new ways of behaving.
2. Ask participants to write down one to three ideas of things that they can do (or have done) and then share with another person (or small group). Have the pairs (or groups) identify one to three ideas that they can then report back to the entire system.
3. Brainstorm things that you can do in your school to celebrate the moral growth exhibited by students. Often recognition goes only to those who continually exhibit positive behaviors. While these students should continue to be recognized, they could also be used as role models and mentors to help other students develop new behaviors.

Other Metaphorical Uses or Parallels

This book can also be used to explore the ways that teachers and staff view their educational leader and what behaviors they value in that person. See activities in *Leading Learning for School Improvement: Using Children's Literature for Professional Dialogue*, by Jacqueline Jacobs and Julie Rotholz.

Illustrations

The illustrations are lovely and provide a strong representation of the principal, student, and others in the school environment. The emotions of the people involved are beautifully depicted and represent the considerations that should be given to solving the problem presented in the book.

Recommended Background Reading

D. Killingbeck, "The Role of Television News in the Construction of School Violence as a Moral Panic," *Journal of Criminal Justice Popular Culture* 8, no. 3 (2000): 186–202.

Insight into Action

Take the ideas generated in discussion question 2 and share them via a newsletter or web pages that may exist for sharing teacher's ideas. For discussion question 3, ask a committee to take the ideas that are generated and develop a plan for the faculty to approve that will acknowledge the contributions of all individuals toward improving the social, emotional, spiritual, and academic environment of the school, particularly efforts that are indicative of altruism.

CULTURE OF VIOLENCE: ACTIVITY 3

Purpose

The purpose of this activity is to consider the relationship between self-esteem issues and school violence.

Materials

- Book: S. Silverstein, *The Missing Piece Meets the Big O* (New York: HarperCollins, 1981). ISBN 0-06-025657-5

Abstract of the Children's Book

The story of the missing piece shows how the search for a place to belong can be strong no matter what your circumstances. The missing piece has a number of adventures along the way and finally manages to feel that he belongs.

Setting the Stage

1. Think about a time when you were excluded from belonging to a group that was important to you, such as not being chosen for a baseball team or not receiving an invitation to an event, such as a party. How did you feel?
2. How likely do you think someone is to seek violence as a way of gaining acceptance? Do we have examples of that in our world today?

Notes on Reading the Book

The book is typical Shel Silverstein, an author most people know best for his poetry collections. The adventures of the missing piece evoke memories of not belonging that most people have felt. However, the events along the way are pretty routine, so read it with a normal voice until the end when the missing piece finally "fits."

Discussion Questions

1. In what ways are the efforts of the missing piece like students who are trying to find a place to belong?
2. Think of one or more examples of peer group rejection that you have witnessed. What do you think would help to mollify the effects of these behaviors?
3. How can the adults in a school be observant and reach out to students to help them find their own identity and to avert violence?

Facilitating the Discussion

1. In spite of the fact that the missing piece did not fit in many places, it was persistent in the effort to belong. Students often exhibit similar behaviors in their efforts to fit in. Some do it overtly, some covertly, and some just "suffer in silence."

2. Ask the participants to write down some details of a peer group rejection they've witnessed. Then have them share commonalities
   among those experiences. What ideas can they generate to eliminate the behaviors in the school environment?
3. Help the group come up with ideas for ways they can increase ob-
   servance of a student's actions that might signal attempts to get
   attention or lead to violence. Most teachers do not want to think
   about the fact that there are students who may act out in order to
   fit in.

Other Metaphorical Uses or Parallels

The story of the missing piece provides another opportunity to think
about students' many creative talents and how they can be used in many
different ways.

Illustrations

The simple line drawings provide a visual for the efforts of the missing piece to find where he belongs. It will not be necessary to share all
of the drawings, but you should identify some that you think will have
particular meaning for your group.

Recommended Background Reading

F. Leach, "Learning to Be Violent: The Role of the School in Developing Adolescent Gendered Behavior," *Compare* 33, no. 3 (2003):
385–401.

Insight into Action

Using discussion question 3 as a basis for decision making, help teachers consider ways that they can support each other in their common efforts to work with students to develop healthy identities and promote
good decision making. Develop a committee that takes responsibility for
monitoring student behavior and actions so that interventions can occur
before acts of violence occur.

HEALTH ISSUES: ACTIVITY I

Purpose

The purpose of this activity is to explore memories and experiences of change and loss due to illness, and to highlight the widely divergent responses individuals make to sickness and disease.

Materials

- Book: A. Ackermann and A. Ackermann, *Our Mom Has Cancer* (Atlanta: American Cancer Society, 2001). ISBN 0-944235-31-X
- Paper and pencils for all participants

Abstract of the Children's Book

Written by two sisters, age nine and eleven, this book chronicles their family's struggle to come to terms with their mother's diagnosis of breast cancer. They acknowledge the ups and downs of the experience, the parts of family life that changed through their mother's treatment, and how the disease affected their lives.

Setting the Stage

Note: Divide the group into small groups of four to six. Ask each member of each group to record the following:

1. A personal experience that you remember as a child regarding loss and change. How did you feel and respond?
2. A personal experience from your adult life regarding loss and change. How did you feel and respond?
3. Examine your answers to the first two questions and make a note of the similarities and differences in your responses to loss at those two points in your life.
4. When each individual completes the exercise in their small groups, discuss the lists to determine if there are similarities in how adults and children respond to loss.

Notes on Reading the Book

Since the narrator of this story is a young girl and the story reads as if written by a female child, a female voice that can project the emotionality of this story is the best choice to read this aloud.

Discussion Questions

Note: The facilitator should pose the following questions when each small group has completed its work.

1. What were the common themes in the stories and perspectives that were shared, either childhood memories or adult experiences?
2. Could you identify common emotions as you discussed your experiences?
3. What has changed since you were a child?
4. What has remained the same?
5. Do we unconsciously overburden students with our own anxiety, memory, and sadness regarding health issues? Is it difficult for you, personally, to remain optimistic in the face of illness and disease?

Facilitating the Discussion

1. For many educators, the memories of diagnoses of loved ones with serious illnesses are terrifying, as prior to modern treatments; cancer was far more often fatal than it is today. How are our own attitudes about illness transferred to students? Are most of you comfortable discussing serious illness with students who may need comfort and support?
2. One's knowledge level of the disease or illness, the type and amount of support, the overall expected prognosis, and the degree of disruption that the illness inflicts can strongly affect individual's emotional responses. How do these variables touch how children and adults, respectively, respond to a medical diagnosis? What sorts of behavior manifestations are you likely to see in students who are experiencing loss and family disruption due to serious illness?

Other Metaphorical Uses or Parallels

This book could also be used to demonstrate family resiliency in the face of crises, and the importance of confronting tough issues in a straightforward and honest way.

Illustrations

The authors, age nine and eleven at the time of publication, also illustrated this book. Although the drawings have emotional appeal, they lack the design sophistication to capture the attention of a large audience. The text, in this case, is a better area to emphasize.

Recommended Background Reading

For cancer information, check the website of the American Cancer Society at www.cancer.org. Other resources to facilitate child–adult conversations regarding illness, disease, and death include S. C. Scholzman, "The Shrink in the Classroom: When Illness Strikes," *Educational Leadership* 60, no. 1 (2002b): 82–83.

Insight into Action

Does your school's social worker or guidance counselor conduct group sessions for students who are experiencing family stress due to serious illness, loss, divorce, or change? If not, is there a need for such student services? If groups are already established, what else can we do to provide support to the school community's families that may need extra help, comfort, or assistance?

HEALTH ISSUES: ACTIVITY 2

Purpose

The purpose of this activity is to help participants examine the different aspects of health issues common in schools. Even when they are as apparently benign as going to the dentist, such events affect our instructional day. Additionally, it provides the opportunity for problem solving when students' academic instruction is affected by health issues.

Materials

- Book: W. Steig, *Doctor De Soto* (New York: Farrar, Straus & Giroux, 1990). ISBN 0-374-41810-1
- Chart paper
- Markers

Abstract of the Children's Book

This book tells the story of a fine dentist (a mouse) who treats patients regardless of their size or dental needs. One day a potentially dangerous patient (a fox) appears at the door. But, because of his dedication to his work and the apparent pain of the fox, the dentist decides to treat him. The story conveys the wickedness of the fox's decision to eat the mice after the treatment. However, the dentist outsmarts the fox after fixing his tooth by making it impossible for him to eat them. This is a delightful story of commitment to work, compassion for others, and problem solving.

Setting the Stage

1. Consider the effects on your daily life when you have to make an appointment to go to the dentist or physician. What effects does it have?
2. Consider the effects on your students when they have to go to dental or medical appointments during the day and miss classes. Write down several effects that you have observed.

Notes on Reading the Book

The book is easy to read and is a cute story of a dedicated dentist and a dilemma that he solves. Read it with appropriate attention to the professionalism of the dentist and the cunning of the fox. Also read the effects of the problem solving of the dentist with pride, but not arrogance.

Discussion Questions

1. The dentist solved a major problem related to his patient, the fox. What problems do you face as an educator when students have to miss school due to medical or dental appointments?
2. Should students be penalized on their grades when they miss a class for medical reasons if they make up the work?
3. Do we have a system in our school that supports students to acquire the knowledge and instruction they may miss due to medical or dental issues? If so, what do we do? If not, what could we do?

Facilitating the Discussion

1. Encourage participants to discuss issues related to missed instructional time, missed tests, and so on. Try to generate as many issues as you can. Record them on chart paper.
2. Ask participants to write down their personal views on whether students should be penalized for time missed from different issues generated in discussion question 1. For example, for "missed instructional time" they might say, "Yes, because my lectures are important information."
3. Brainstorm ideas on how students are supported when they have to deal with medical or dental needs or emergencies. Take an issue as identified above in discussion question 2 and think of ways that the student could avoid penalties. For example, for "missed instructional time" if the lecture is important, it could be taped, or a student could be asked to take notes to share with a student who is absent.

Other Metaphorical Uses or Parallels

This book can be used to generate strategies to problem solve issues in schools.

Illustrations

The illustrations are cute, simple color drawings that convey the challenges the dentist faced in trying to serve a wide range of patients, but also his willingness to problem solve.

Recommended Background Reading

B. E. Compas and M. C. Boyer, "Coping and Attention: Implications for Child Health and Pediatric Conditions," *Journal of Developmental and Behavioral Pediatrics* 22, no. 5 (2001): 323–34.

Insight into Action

Use the ideas from discussion question 3 to help teachers start to move to a view of differentiating instruction so that students are *not* penalized for missing school due to illness. Many students have health issues that are not of their doing or choosing, and all teachers should have a plan for how they can help students during those times.

HEALTH ISSUES: ACTIVITY 3

Purpose

The purpose of this activity is to address the ways that faculty can be involved in supporting students facing personal health problems through understanding and involvement.

Materials

- Book: Y. Peterseil, *Princess Alopecia* (New York: Pitspopany, 1999). ISBN 0-943706-26-2

Abstract of the Children's Book

This book shares the story of a child who has alopecia, or loss of hair, which is a little understood condition. Over 4 million people in the

United States have alopecia and it occurs without warning. The story shows how a caring teacher can help a child gain acceptance and strength during a major health event.

Setting the Stage

1. Have you, or someone you know, had to deal with a student's major health problem? What condition was it? What was the outcome?
2. Have you thought about what you would do if a student in one of your classes had a major illness or health event that caused him or her to miss a lot of school or to appear different?

Notes on Reading the Book

Read through the book so that you can determine the various emotional states that Alopecia experiences, including the attention she received for her beautiful hair to the support she received from others when she lost her hair.

Discussion Questions

1. How would you address the needs of a student with serious health issues without violating his or her right to privacy?
2. What life lessons can students learn from activities related to helping a classmate through a difficult health issue?
3. Is there a plan in school for helping all of the students address and deal with a serious health issue?

Facilitating the Discussion

1. First you need to ensure that faculty realize that a student (and his or her parents by extension) have a right to privacy. If a parent (or student) shares that a major health issue will affect the student's looks, actions, or attendance, what are the ways that parents could be asked to help inform other students so that they can be supportive? This might include asking the parent to sign a release to

allow the teacher to share minimal information, or asking the parent or student to speak to the class or a subset of students.

2. Students, even if they cannot be informed about a particular student's health issue, may benefit from discussing what/how they would respond if faced with a serious health issue. Discuss the ways that this could happen without taking time from instruction. For example, there are certainly pieces of literature at all age levels that present issues of health that could be read and discussed.

3. Invite teachers to review and revise, if needed, policies or plans that address health concerns. If there is not a plan, the development of one can help allay fears that faculty may have about what to do if faced with a student's serious health issue.

Other Metaphorical Uses or Parallels

This book can also be used to discuss disabilities that result in an individual looking different from others.

Illustrations

The colorful illustrations provide a fairy-tale experience in the life of Princess Alopecia, her emotion in losing her hair, and also in the support she receives from her teacher and fellow classmates.

Recommended Background Reading

L. S. Walker, J. Garber, C. Smith, D. A. VanSlyke, and R. L. Claar, "The Relation of Daily Stressors to Somatic and Emotional Symptoms in Children with and without Recurrent Abdominal Pain," *Journal of Consulting Clinical Psychology* 69 (2001): 85–91.

Insight into Action

From discussion question 3, be sure that any plan that is in place, or devised, is regularly reviewed and that all faculty know that they can/should recommend ways to improve the plan. As more students exhibit allergies (e.g., peanuts) there can be serious discussions necessary to ensure that teachers and staff are prepared to respond if needed and a safe learning environment is always provided.

PEER PRESSURE: ACTIVITY I

Purpose

The purpose of this activity is to acknowledge the persistence and timelessness of peer pressure and to understand the positive and negative effects it has on student behavior.

Materials

- Book: I. Livingston, *Finklehopper Frog* (Berkeley, CA: Tricycle, 2003). ISBN 1-58246-075-2

Abstract of the Children's Book

Finklehopper Frog is an amphibian who decides that he wants to join the jogging crowd. First, he searches for and finds the "perfect" outfit for his new endeavor. Much to his chagrin, not only do other animals make fun of his jogging suit, but they ridicule his inability to run. It is only after a rabbit acknowledges his uniqueness does Finklehopper recognize what a gift his individuality really is, and that everyone's special talents deserve to be recognized and appreciated.

Setting the Stage

1. As a child, how were you influenced by your friends? Note specific events or behaviors that you now realize were shaped largely by your peer group. Were you aware of this influence at the time?
2. As an adolescent, how were you influenced by your friends? Note specific events or behaviors that you now realize were shaped largely by your peer group. Were you aware of this influence at the time?
3. Now that you are an adult, how do your friends and peers influence you? Note: When individuals are finished responding to the

questions, divide the group into clusters of five or six. Decide in your small group if you have any experiences in common.

Notes on Reading the Book

This story is told in rhyme, so the best choice of a reader is one who is comfortable using the lilting rhythm and playfulness of this text.

Discussion Questions

1. Look at your responses to the questions posed in the Setting the Stage activity. Which behaviors would you label as growth producing, productive, or beneficial? Did anyone list positive behaviors, or were most of the activities you discussed in your small groups negative?
2. Were any of the behaviors you discussed silly or dangerous? At what age were these behaviors most likely to occur? Did some behaviors resemble bullying?
3. As you discussed your responses in your small groups, did you notice any patterns or similarities based on gender? Does peer pressure have differential effects on boys and girls?
4. Which of the activities that you noted were superficial? Which were substantive?
5. Was one question of the Setting the Stage activity more difficult to answer than the others? Why?
6. Did anyone notice that those who poked fun at Finklehopper were themselves "imperfect"?

Facilitating the Discussion

1. The use of humor is particularly appropriate in facilitating this discussion. All of us have been embarrassed by our occasional (or commonplace) decisions to follow the crowd. Emphasize the reality that we are often compelled to do positive things because those important to us are engaged in such activities, and we never outgrow the need to be accepted by our peers.
2. Often, as adults, we are not fully aware of the degree to which we are molded and shaped by others. As participants discuss the com-

monalities of their experiences, stress the point that we are social creatures, and part of who we are is what others tell us about ourselves. We're shaped by the behaviors and attitudes of the peers with whom we choose to associate.

3. In regard to comments that reflect negative influences, ask if the participant was fully aware of the consequences of those activities or actions at the time. Note that even today, we may not be fully cognizant of the full effects others have on us and our actions.

4. Throughout the discussion, guide participants toward a greater understanding of and empathy for students who seem overly shaped in a negative way by peer pressure. Have traditional interventions worked, either in your classroom or throughout the school as a whole? Do adult reprimands and cautions typically reduce the reliance on peers? Did it work for you?

Other Metaphorical Uses or Parallels

This book could be used to facilitate a discussion about special education, diversity, multiculturalism, or inclusion.

Illustrations

The pictures in this book are detailed and complex; it's easy to skip over some that are particularly rich and meaningful. The illustration on the last page of the book includes a caterpillar in a wheelchair, a frog pushing a polliwog in a carriage, and a worm hopping on a pogo stick; all are indicative of the need to be welcoming and accepting of those who think and behave differently than the majority.

Recommended Background Reading

M. K. Meyerhoff, "Peer Pressure Protection," *Pediatrics for Parents* 18, no. 7 (1999): 8.

Insight into Action

Make note of any opportunities for student-directed appreciation of differences that are present at your school—appreciation for differences and the ability to make informed choices about the extent to which, if at all, one wishes to follow the crowd. These are important skills for students to learn, no matter what their age.

After all, the last line of the book states, "There's room for everyone." Is this true at your school? If not, why not? Devise a strategy through which an appreciation for diversity and difference becomes part of the school culture, not merely something that gets lip service. This is particularly true for adolescent girls, since negative messages from peers can result in life-threatening behaviors.

PEER PRESSURE: ACTIVITY 2

Purpose

The purpose of this activity is to examine ways that students put pressure on each other and how teachers and staff promote and encourage student acceptance.

Materials

- Book: K. Hankes, *Chrysanthemum* (New York: Green Willow, 2000). ISBN 0-688-09699-9

Abstract of the Children's Book

Chrysanthemum is a sweet little girl who is excited about going to school until her peers convince her that school is not for her. The influence of a caring teacher helps her see that she is stronger than the influence presented by her peers.

Setting the Stage

1. Think about how you feel when you hear colleagues criticize a peer or pressure her to adopt their point of view.
2. Do you think you are influenced in your own perceptions of yourself by how your peers act toward you?

3. Are you influenced by a person's name? Ahmed, Adolf, Sunshine, Consuela?

Notes on Reading the Book

This book is so delightful in the spirit of the little mouse named Chrysanthemum. Read through the book so you can think about how the inflection in your voice might best represent each of the characters. Be sure that you (or the reader you choose) can adequately convey hostility, teasing, sadness, and joy.

Discussion Questions

1. List the changes you have noticed in a student's behavior that appear with no apparent antecedent event. Share with one or two other teachers at your table and decide on one or two that you think are examples of dramatic changes.
2. Are there ways that you can tell that peer pressure is part of the change in a student's behavior? How could you discover a behavioral changes cause, since students are generally reluctant to share such information?
3. What positive uses of peer pressure can we develop for our school?

Facilitating the Discussion

1. If teachers need examples, share one that you have observed (e.g., the star football player who suddenly loses interest in winning). Move around as teachers are sharing and help them to refine their ideas to come up with one or two that are examples of dramatic change.
2. Probably the most critical element here is to help teachers think about the importance of observation. Just watching students as they interact in the halls, at lunch, before or after school provide information about what may be happening. Discuss the importance of developing trust with students so that they feel that they can come to you when they are feeling pressured.
3. Help teachers generate a list of positive uses of peer pressure (e.g., group benefits from the high school band winning state marching

band competition earns everyone the chance to attend a demonstration of the band's work on a Friday afternoon.)

Other Metaphorical Uses or Parallels

The emphasis on unique characteristics, whether a name, an ability to speak more than one language, a physical characteristic, talent or personality trait, can be celebrated and shared among students and teachers.

Illustrations

The clearly happy child shown on pages 1–6 is quickly depicted as demoralized by peer rejection on page 7. Highlight the disillusionment that is evident in Chrysanthemum's face on pages 8–10 as she is hurt by her peers. Point out the use of the illustration to represent the transformation in Chrysanthemum that is brought about by the support provided by her music teacher on page 27.

Recommended Background Reading

G. W. Ladd, "Peer Relationships and Social Competence during Early and Middle Childhood," *Annual Review of Psychology,* 1999, 1–30, www.findarticles.com/cfdis/m0961/1999.Annual/544442303/print.jhtml.

Insight into Action

Develop a committee of teachers and parents to look at ways that positive peer pressure can be used effectively in the school. Also develop ways that students can be taught to cope with negative peer pressure and identify adult or peer role models who can be of assistance when students are struggling with negative peer pressure.

PEER PRESSURE: ACTIVITY 3

Purpose

The purpose of this activity is to see the positive effect of peer pressure. Often educators and parents perceive peer pressure as a bad thing.

This is an opportunity to look at ways that peer pressure can bring happiness to the individual and growth in others.

Materials

- Book: K. Wilson, *Hilda Must Be Dancing* (New York: Simon & Schuster Children's Publishing Division, 2004). ISBN 0-689-84788-2

Abstract of the Children's Book

This delightful book tells the story of Hilda the hippo who loves to dance. There's a major problem because her dancing makes so much noise that the other animals can't think or do anything when she is dancing. Her friends want her to find another hobby. She can't imagine anything else that she could do that would be as much fun as dancing. Finally through the positive pressure of peers, she finds that there is a way she can dance and be accepted by her peers.

Setting the Stage

1. Quickly write down three words that come to mind when you hear the words "peer pressure."
2. Can you think of an example of peer pressure that you have witnessed lately? Write it down quickly.

Notes on Reading the Book

The book requires a reader who is willing to "dance" while reading and "make music" of the words. There is so much power in the language of the book and the fun that comes from watching Hilda do something she loves and then finding a way to do that and grow as a result of the positive pressure of others.

Discussion Questions

1. Was the peer pressure exerted on Hilda positive or negative? In what way?

2. Do we limit our thinking about peer pressure to its negative aspects and consequences? If so, does this limit our ability to use peer pressure in a positive way in our classes and school?
3. What strategies can you use to effect change in student behavior through the positive use of peer pressure?

Facilitating the Discussion

1. Help participants realize that the pressure is positive because even though her friends didn't like the noise she made, they honored her desire to express herself through dancing. The water buffalo helped her to find herself through swimming.
2. Participants can quickly identify ways that peer pressure is viewed as negative (e.g., students who start smoking because of peer pressure, students who are capable of good academic achievement but do not perform because of peer pressure). Discuss ways that the adults can shift their thinking to consider types of peer pressure that can be good and productive.
3. Ask participants to write down one or two of their ideas for positive uses of peer pressure and how they can facilitate the idea's adoption. Coaches are often great sources of ideas for this activity. The idea here is to get people to think about positive outcomes from the peer pressure. Once they have written down one or two ideas, ask them to share so you can discuss several of them. At the end of the activity, all ideas should be recorded and shared.

Other Metaphorical Uses or Parallels

This book is also excellent for discussing issues related to creativity and self-expression.

Illustrations

The illustrations are bright, colorful paintings that have such delightful imagery that you will want to share them to help participants think creatively and positively about ways that they can encourage and develop positive peer pressure.

Recommended Background Reading

Peer pressure information and materials are available from Scholastic at www.scholastic.com/schoolage/grade5/development/5_copingpeerpress. htm.

Insight into Action

Share the ideas generated in discussion question 3 through posting them on your web page or providing hard copies to all teachers. You could develop a reading circle that would find and share a book that one of your faculty members has found to be particularly provocative on the effects of positive peer pressure.

EQUALITY AND FAIRNESS: ACTIVITY I

Purpose

The purpose of this activity is to help teachers understand that although we may all agree that equity is important, we may disagree about precisely what constitutes fair and equitable, particularly when we don't control the criteria on which decisions will be made. Teachers are urged to look beyond their own experiences with equity to examine the issue of school funding at the macro level.

Materials

- Book: J. Stevens, *Tops and Bottoms* (New York: Scholastic, 1995). ISBN 0-590-86496-3
- Paper and pencils or pens for each participant

Abstract of the Children's Book

A pair of longtime rivals, the hare and the bear, enter into a business agreement devised by the hare. The hare agrees to do all of the work of planting and harvesting if he can use the bear's land. The bear agrees, but no matter the choices he makes regarding which part of the harvest will be his, he always loses out to the cunning of the hare. When the bear chooses the tops of the crops, the hare plants beets, carrots, and radishes. The pair struggle through three planting seasons before the bear finally realizes that he can't win.

Setting the Stage

1. Write a paragraph about an event or incident in which you believe you were not treated fairly.
2. Did you control the criteria that determined the distribution of the goods, decision, or event in question?
3. Were the criteria clear in your mind?
4. How do issues of equity and fairness affect debates in education? What are the current concerns about equity in your district or state?

Notes on Reading the Book

This is an emotionally laden book, particularly the voice of the bear who, no matter what he chooses, finds himself on the losing end of his deals with the hare. The best reader for this book is someone who can bellow the indignation of the bear, as well as the cool confidence of the hare.

Discussion Questions

1. Why is it important to understand the basic criteria on which questions of equitable distribution will be determined?
2. Why are we more sensitive to being treated unfairly when it doesn't benefit us than we are when we're treated unfairly, but the treatment is in our favor?
3. How do students in your classes define and understand fairness in education?
4. Do you routinely talk with students about how grades, for example, are determined and the precise criteria that will determine their grades?

Facilitating the Discussion

1. We all agree that people should be treated fairly. Equity is generally defined as "treating likes alike." However, assume a student earns a 78 on a test with 100 points. Depending on the criteria chosen, that score may be an A (if graded on a curve; it may be the highest score in the class), a B (if graded on a scale determined by the mean score), or a C (if the grade is determined by a predetermined raw score distribution). Thus, the criterion on which the grade is based determines the final grade. This is but one example of "whosoever determines the criteria has the power." This simple truism is the underlying point of this exercise.

2. As the participants share their experiences of inequitable distributions, monitor the affect expressed. Issues of equity and fairness are fundamental to individual's feelings of self-worth, motivation, and sense of power in an organization. The same is true for students. Although teachers may be sensitive to issues of equity that affect them (such as merit pay), the same teachers may be unaware of how their actions and decisions, which seem commonsense to them, are perceived far differently (and as unfair) by students. This conversation can take many paths. Certainly, on a large scale, questions of equity, particularly regarding funding at the state level, have plagued educators and policy makers since the founding of public education. Who should get what? What are the criteria on which distributions are based? What are the underlying assumptions inherent in the ground rules? Why are questions of equity so value loaded?

3. As you talk with participants, help them understand that "where you stand depends on where you sit." This is particularly true regarding equity "in the process" versus equity "in the result."

Other Metaphorical Uses or Parallels

This book can be used for discussion on conflict resolution, power and politics in organizations, or to stimulate conversations about merit versus need in societal benefits.

Illustrations

This book is a Caldecott Honor Book, and when you see the pictures, you'll understand why. The illustrations are both playful and powerful. The format of the book (which is not evident by its cover) is vertical rather than horizontal.

Recommended Background Reading

B. J. Biddle and D. C. Berliner, "Unequal School Funding in the United States," *Educational Leadership* 59, no. 8 (2002): 48–59; D. Stone, *Policy, Paradox, and Political Reason* (New York: Scott, Foresman, 1988).

Insight into Action

To fight the continuing inequities in school funding, teachers must have accurate data at their fingertips to counter the unsupportable claims about the effects of inequitable school funding. Find and distribute current data from the National Center for Education Statistics and the Rockefeller Foundation, which routinely funds and distributes research on education and equity. In addition, find ways to become more politically active, whether or not you currently teach in a school that receives inadequate funds. Politicians and policy makers are often woefully unaware of the real conditions in schools. If you do teach in a school that is underfunded, scour the literature to find strategies that have been associated with greater student achievement, such as finding, motivating, and retaining the best-qualified teachers, and work hard to reduce class size (Biddle and Berliner 2002).

EQUALITY AND FAIRNESS: ACTIVITY 2

Purpose

The purpose of this activity is to help participants discuss the value that each individual places in his or her upbringing and to examine the ways that individuals may see fairness in their lives.

Materials

- Book: F. Ringgold, *Tar Beach* (New York: Crown, 1991). ISBN 0-517-58030-6

Abstract of the Children's Book

This story is a powerful message from a child who believes that all things are possible if you dream them. Even though she grew up in an inner city with parents who worked hard but were not part of the local establishment, she learned the value of belief in herself and others. Her beach was as real to her as any sandy beach visited by another.

Setting the Stage

1. Think of a family experience you had as a child that you later learned was very different from other families' experiences.
2. Think of one dream that you had for your future from which no one could dissuade you.

Notes on Reading the Book

The book should be read in a voice that conveys all the power and strength of a child who honors her heritage and believes that all things are possible if you dream. This is a book of hope and strength.

Discussion Questions

1. How is the life of the little girl in this book like (or unlike) the lives of children or young people in this school?
2. Write two ways that you, as a teacher, draw on the heritage of students in your class to help them compare their lives to the material they are studying in your class.
3. What are some specific strategies that could be used to integrate the heritage of your students with the everyday curriculum of the students you teach?

Facilitating the Discussion

1. Using their responses to discussion question 1, help participants find ways that they are similar (or not) by responding to (or soliciting) such ideas as "hopeful," "creative," "has dreams," "accepting." For instance, the little girl did not know that her "beach" was not the same beach that others might have and found things that she loved about it. As facilitator, be prepared to share a personal experience of a student who has shown that ability if no one volunteers one.

2. Ask the participants to write down two ways that they draw on the heritage of their students to make their class work relevant. Have them turn those in so that you can use them to develop an Insight into Action project.

3. Using the ideas generated in discussion question 2, ask the teachers to work in pairs or small groups to generate (or share) specific strategies for their grade level or subject area.

Other Metaphorical Uses or Parallels

This book can also be used to discuss the influence of parents who set examples for their children through hard work and belief in their ability to do anything.

Illustrations

The illustrations are taken from a quilt series, done by the author, which is in the collection of the Solomon R. Guggenheim Museum in New York City. They are colorful and bright and tell the story themselves.

Recommended Background Reading

D. DeCremer, "Effects of Roles and Performance Feedback on the Equality Rule in Resource-Sharing Tasks," *Journal of Social Psychology* 141, no. 1 (2001): 153.

Insight into Action

From the ideas generated in discussion question 3, ask each group to collate the ideas and come up with a list of strategies that teachers in your particular school are using and which have been successful with your students. You can share this information in the form of a resource notebook to which new ideas could be added, an idea page on your website, and so on.

EQUALITY AND FAIRNESS: ACTIVITY 3

Purpose

The purpose of this activity is to provide a forum for discussing issues related to equality and fairness. Even though bad things happen in life, one of the hallmarks of education is to help children and young people, and even educators, to have hope.

Materials

- Book: E. Jackson, *Sometimes Bad Things Happen* (Brookfield, CT: Millbrook, 2002). ISBN 0-7613-2810-6

Abstract of the Children's Book

This book provides a poignant walk through the bad things and emotions that one can feel in life. It was written following 9/11 and though the focus is not that world tragedy, it conveys emotion that is real, no matter what the circumstances, when we experience "bad things" or don't understand why "bad things" happen.

Setting the Stage

1. Take a moment to reflect on something "bad" that has happened to you, or in our world, or to someone you know. Consider the emotions that you experienced during that event.
2. Now think about what you did (or do) to cope with those emotions.

Notes on Reading the Book

This book is easy to read, but requires a voice that can express a range of emotions. It is important to express the sadness, fear, and regret that is evident in the words of the author. But, it is also important to be able to shift that voice and convey the hope that is evident at the end of the book.

Discussion Questions

1. What aspects of this book provided the most significant emotions for you?
2. Think of a student (or students) with whom you have worked that experienced a particularly bad or difficult time. What was your reaction? Could you discuss what was unfair about the experience?
3. What strategies do faculty employ, individually and collectively, to help ourselves and others cope during difficult times?

Facilitating the Discussion

1. Give the participants a few minutes to reflect on their personal response to the book. Call on several people who are willing to share their response. Discuss the range of emotions that people have witnessed in difficult times (e.g., 9/11; assassination of President John F. Kennedy).
2. Ask the participants not to identify the student by name, but rather to discuss their *own* reaction to the event/situation. Did they find it difficult to relate to the student? Were they able to consider "fairness and equality" in the situation? (E.g., was it fair that many people who went to work on 9/11 were killed and others stopped to get coffee and were spared?)
3. Ask participants to take a few minutes to write down strategies that they use to help students cope in difficult times. Then have them pair/share and turn in their ideas so that they can be collated and shared with others.

Other Metaphorical Uses or Parallels

This book could also be used to discuss issues related to death, divorce, and loss.

Illustrations

The photography for this book is clear, poignant, and realistic. The photographer's dedication is "To everyone who lives who will never be the same after September 11th." Her photographs represent the range of our emotions when faced with "bad times" and yet provide a beautiful framework for the belief that good does happen, too.

Recommended Background Reading

P. Perlmutter, "Double Standards, Double Talk, and Multiple Troubles," *Independent Review* 5, no. 2 (2000): 313.

Insight into Action

Collect the strategies generated in discussion question 3 and compile them into a document that can be shared with faculty. Then follow up in a subsequent discussion about how these strategies can be used collectively and what is important in a school emergency plan that reaches beyond the immediate response to the after effects. Share the results of those strategies with the faculty and decide on several that can be included in the faculty handbook.

EFFECTS OF MEDIA: ACTIVITY I

Purpose

The purpose of this activity is to examine the ways that children can misinterpret the library media available. It also includes discussion of ways to increase student participation in reading and helping them to assess the influence of various media.

Materials

- Book: M. Thaler, *The Librarian from the Black Lagoon* (New York: Scholastic, 1997). ISBN 0-590-50311-1

Abstract of the Children's Book

The book provides an interesting view of student perceptions about what happens in a media center. They think that the books are bolted together and that the librarian laminates anyone who talks. Their perceptions are proved wrong when they enter the media center and find the librarian is a nice person who wants them to read.

Setting the Stage

1. What do you do to prepare students for using the media center in your school?
2. What considerations do you give to assignments that may require students to go to the public library where materials are not as tightly controlled as they are in a school media center?

Notes on Reading the Book

The book is an easy read and provides a great framework for assessing student perceptions of what happens in a media center. The "voice bubbles" are a great way to add humor. You might want to have more than one person involved in the reading.

Discussion Questions

1. Consider what you think students need to know to be effective users of the media center. Identify several things that you can share with others.
2. What are the limitations from a student's point of view of the materials available in the media center? Are these really limitations or do we need to develop their abilities to use these media?
3. How can you improve the use of media in learning about concepts or ideas in your subject area or a subject area you teach?

Facilitating the Discussion

1. Ask participants to list their ideas and share those among the group.
2. Consider the available resources in your own media center and see what issues or concerns arise. Are there materials or resources that are seldom used? Does the media specialist provide information to faculty about new materials and resources and ways that they can be used?
3. Ask teachers to pair/share or in small groups discuss the ways that they can improve the use of media. Encourage them to discuss issues that can arise if assigned topics are either too broad or do not require the teacher's approval. For example, topic ambiguity can lead to a student selecting a topic that the teacher had not anticipated and is not prepared to discuss.

Other Metaphorical Uses or Parallels

This book can be used to discuss students' feelings about any of the adults in the school whom they do not see on a regular basis.

Illustrations

The illustrations are humorous and cartoonlike. The exaggeration adds to the believability of the misperceptions that students can have about adults in their environment with whom they do not have continuous contact.

Recommended Background Reading

Media violence and effects on the American family: Baby Bag Online (www.babybag.com/articles/amaviol.htm).

Insight into Action

Provide opportunities for teachers to discuss ways that they can continue to share ideas about the use and effects of media. If there is not a system in place for the media specialist to inform teachers of new materials and resources, create a group to consult with the media specialist to decide how that can best be provided.

EFFECTS OF MEDIA: ACTIVITY 2

Purpose

The purpose of this activity is to allow teachers to have a discussion on the effects of media on values and daily decisions.

Materials

- Book: D. McPhail, *Mole Music* (New York: Holt, 1999). ISBN 0-8050-2819-6

Abstract of the Children's Book

This book tells the story of a mole who spent all day underground digging tunnels but spent his nights watching television. He was so strongly influenced by an ad on television one night that he bought a product that changed his life forever.

Setting the Stage

1. Think of an ad you have seen on television that you can describe or recite without thinking about it.
2. Has this ad positively or negatively influenced you? In what way has it influenced you?

Notes on Reading the Book

Read the humdrum routine of the mole's life in digging every day and watching television every night. Show interest in your voice when he responds to the advertisement. Use strong expressions of hope when reading what he believes will happen from his music. Show contentment when he realizes that his music won't have the effects of his dreams, but it does bring him peace.

Discussion Questions

1. How are students' lives affected by the media and the shows and advertisements that they see?

2. Is it possible for the instructional program of a school to bring the same kind of enthusiam to students that they experience in watching television? Why or why not?
3. Is there a need for a specific curriculum in school to help students be objective consumers of the media that they watch or read?

Facilitating the Discussion

1. Ask participants to discuss their perceptions of how students are affected by the media, including such things as clothing, hair styles, and language.
2. Prompt teachers to share ideas on how to engage students in learning when they are accustomed to fast paced, highly visual and strongly influenced sound effects media. This might include using media, when appropriate, music, lots of descriptive language, or a wide variety of instructional strategies.
3. Examine the current offerings in your school and look at whether consumerism is being taught through current courses. If not, discussions can be held to determine in what ways students can connect the substantive content of common media and the style in which it is delivered.

Other Metaphorical Uses or Parallels

This book can be used to look at self-confidence as exhibited by the mole once he started making music.

Illustrations

The illustrations provide a colorful image of the underground world in which the mole lives and the world above ground that influences the mole. The imagery of the effect of his music is evident in the trees.

Recommended Background Reading

A. I. Nathanson, "Parents versus Peers: Exploring the Significance of Peer Mediation of Antisocial Television," *Communication Research* 28, no. 3 (2001): 251–75.

Insight into Action

Follow up on how teachers can and do use media to help students engage in the learning process and to identify how they are influenced by it. This can be done by soliciting feedback by e-mail or by setting up a group that will identify components of media in different subject areas and how they use it.

EFFECTS OF MEDIA: ACTIVITY 3

Purpose

The purpose of this activity is to prompt a discussion among participants on how media is used in schools.

Materials

- Book: J. Scieszka, *The True Story of the Three Little Pigs* (New York: Viking, 1989). ISBN 0-67082759-2

Abstract of the Children's Book

This is the story of the three little pigs told from the wolf's perspective. He provides a plausible reason for why the houses were destroyed and why he ate the pigs. In the end he believes he was framed.

Setting the Stage

1. Do you think it is legitimate to have students using the Internet to find material for learning activities?
2. Is the information that students find on the Internet reliable? Truthful? Accurate?

Notes on Reading the Book

This book provides the opportunity to use a great voice as a confident wolf who is so sure that his side of the story has not been heard and that when heard, he will be understood. Use animation and confidence in reading it.

Discussion Questions

1. If there are two sides to the story of the three little pigs, is it reasonable to think there are two sides to most information that is provided in schools?
2. In what ways are the issues of "who" is telling the story a concern for the use of various media in the classroom?
3. What skills do you teach students to help them be good consumers of information from the media?

Facilitating the Discussion

1. Help participants think through the many examples that can be generated relative to the perspective from which information is provided. This might include consideration that we have gone through several different strategies for the "best" way to teach mathematics.
2. There are, and have been, many concerns that some subjects are particularly biased to a certain perspective and point of view. Most notable in this regard are omissions of women, minorities, and certain political points of view from history books. Help participants think of how they provide a balance when the materials with which they work are focused on a particular group to the exclusion of the contributions of another.
3. Have individuals identify specific strategies (for example, write them down) they use and then share those among the group. Look for commonalities and ways that the strategies can be incorporated in a schoolwide effort to reinforce good consumer strategies.

Other Metaphorical Uses or Parallels

This book can be used to help students consider their ability to take a well-known writing and tell it from a different perspective. The effects of this on creative development can be quite strong.

Illustrations

Bright colors and animated expressions make the illustrations in this book delightful to share. You can engender real support for the wolf through sharing the illustrations.

Recommended Background Reading

J. W. Loewen, *Lies My Teacher Told Me: Everything Your American History Textbook Got Wrong* (New York: New Press of the City University of New York, 1995).

Insight into Action

Based on the discussion in questions 2 and 3, share information with all teachers so that there is benefit from the ideas that have been identified. Use these to address the issue of the media and good consumerism with it.

EFFECTS OF MEDIA: ACTIVITY 4

Purpose

The purpose of this activity is to help participants examine the media hype that surrounds the world of professional athletics and the effect it has on the educational experiences of young men and women. Despite the downside of professional sports, this activity notes the importance of having a dream and working toward it.

Materials

- Book: D. Jordan and R. M. Jordan, *Salt in His Shoes* (New York: Simon & Schuster, 2000). ISBN 0-689-83371-7

Abstract of the Children's Book

The book shares the story of Michael Jordan, who has had a great deal of media coverage in his lifetime. The story in the book, however, is about how a young Michael wanted to play basketball and wanted to be good at it. He looked to his family for support and followed his mother's advice. The emphasis in the story is on believing in yourself and working hard to achieve your goals.

Setting the Stage

1. Identify one thing in your life that was important for you to achieve. What did you do to achieve it?
2. Think of one of your students who is working hard to achieve a personal goal. What are the characteristics of this student?

Notes on Reading the Book

This book should be read with consideration for the early Michael when he is unsure of himself and disappointed in his inability to play as well as his older brothers and their friends because of what he believes about his height. The parents' voices should reflect the acceptance and encouragement that they offer him. Read the last page with recognition for his confidence, but not cockiness.

Discussion Questions

1. Has the extensive media coverage of the events in Michael Jordan's life changed him from the young man depicted in the book?
2. Does the media coverage of Michael Jordan provide an opportunity to show children and young people the good that can come from practice, effort, and commitment to a dream?
3. In what ways could you, as a teacher, use positive media to help students examine the world in which we live and the power in believing in one's dreams?

Facilitating the Discussion

1. Facilitate a discussion on the different types of media coverage people have seen of Michael Jordan (e.g., NBA games, ads, interviews, coverage of his father's funeral). In general, you should be able to get consensus that the media coverage has not dramatically

changed his determination to be the best at what he does nor made him arrogant.

2. Help participants consider the limitations we place on children and young people when we fail to use current media figures that are positive to help them examine who they are and where they are headed in life.

3. Ask individuals to write ideas for using media and then share those either orally or place on chart paper.

Other Metaphorical Uses or Parallels

This book can also be used to discuss the ways in which goal setting and working to achieve a goal can be worthwhile.

Illustrations

The oil paintings used for this book provide a beautifully realistic representation of a family working to achieve goals in their day-to-day lives.

Recommended Background Reading

M. Preboth, "Effects of Mass Media Exposure in Children," *American Family Physician* 61, no. 3 (2000): 890.

Insight into Action

Gather the ideas generated in discussion question 3 and post them in the teacher resource section of your website, or generate a list and share it with all teachers. Periodically check with teachers to add new ideas and to share how the use of media has had a positive influence on students.

ECONOMIC UNCERTAINTIES: ACTIVITY I

Purpose

The purpose of this activity is to help teachers explore ways that they can teach, assist, and support students who share the responsibility of providing for their families in times of economic need.

Materials

- Book: C. Hawkins and J. Hawkins, *Fairytale News* (Cambridge, MA: Candlewick, 2004). ISBN 0-7636-2166-8

Abstract of the Children's Book

This delightful book takes some of the best known fairy tales and combines them into a media blitz. The purpose of this unusual twist is to tell the tale of a creative little boy who saves his family from starvation.

Setting the Stage

1. How many families with children are homeless in our community?
2. What actions have you taken to understand the effects of homelessness on students in school?

Notes on Reading the Book

Read the book with despair in the beginning to indicate the depths of poverty that Jack and his mother face. Share the excitement he has when he gets a job delivering the newspaper, which allows him to earn money so the family can eat. Use consternation in your voice for Jack's reaction when the mother criticizes him for what he perceived to be a good exchange with the fast-talking stranger. Show excitement at the end when they all live happily ever after.

Discussion Questions

1. How does the combination of fairy tales contribute to the relationships among the characters in the story?
2. How are the interactions of these characters similar to what happens to children when they are facing the adult realities of poverty and/or homelessness?
3. What strategies can you identify for providing support to students who are homeless and in need of assistance in order to be successful in school?

Facilitating the Discussion

1. For this question, it is important to help the participants consider that each connection of a fairy tale contributed to Jack's ultimate success in providing assistance to his family. So, the relationships were paramount to his success.
2. Help the participants focus on the fact that the resources available to middle class people in our society are not available to people who are homeless and/or living in poverty. Children often feel that they have to do something to help out, even if the adult(s) do not ask for assistance. Children often steal, beg, or try to acquire things that they do not have in order to help out.
3. The focus of discussion question 3 is the importance of developing relationships with students and particularly the acceptance of students, no matter the circumstances in which they live. Consider the community resources that can be garnered to provide things such as school supplies, materials, or after-school tutoring.

Other Metaphorical Uses or Parallels

The use of this book to examine the effects of media would be particularly interesting since the framework for the media is fairy tales.

Illustrations

The illustrations are exaggerations of the well-known fairy tales, and the "bubble voices" provide great insight into how the actions are being perceived.

Recommended Background Reading

B. Raban and C. Ure, *Literacy in the Preschool* (1999). ERIC Document ED 445317. Available at www.eduref.org.

Insight into Action

It is critical for teachers to have the data to understand the number of homeless children served in your community. There may be actions to take to determine how best to assist these students. If there are no homeless in the community served by your school district, there can be discussion of ways that your school community might help a neighboring community that does serve students who are homeless.

ECONOMIC UNCERTAINTIES: ACTIVITY 2

Purpose

The purpose of this book is to explore the effects of being homeless on students and their performance in school.

Materials

* Book: T. Rabe, *The Fish's Tale* (New York: Random House, 2003). ISBN 0-375-82490-1

Abstract of the Children's Book

This simple children's story shares the consequences for a fish when he is displaced from his home by the Cat in the Hat. While the book shares the antics of the Cat in the Hat, the focus is on the fish who is out of his natural habitat. In the end, the fish is returned to his home, but things are never quite the same.

Setting the Stage

1. How much value do you place on having a home that you consider your own?
2. Would you be upset if you were suddenly moved out of your house and made to live somewhere not of your choosing?

Notes on Reading the Book

Read the book in typical Dr. Seuss fashion with focus on the rhyming and rhythm of the language. Be sure to emphasize those aspects that show the fish's concern about being out of his home and the changes that are taking place around him.

Discussion Questions

1. How is the fish out of water like a child who is suddenly homeless?
2. What things about being homeless do you think a child would first find interesting? What things would she or he find scary? What things would be disconcerting?
3. What activities can the faculty in school participate in that will help to better understand the effects of homelessness on a family?

Facilitating the Discussion

1. Discussion here should center around being out of the environment in which she or he has the most experience. Even when a child has not had many material things, if there is uncertainty of where the child will sleep, he or she can feel like a fish out of water.
2. Divide the group into three groups and have each group take one of the elements of discussion question 2: interesting, scary, disconcerting. Ask them to list the things that they come up with and write their ideas on poster paper. Then share with the whole group.
3. Direct the group to brainstorm activities that could be done to better understand the effects of homelessness. This might include a reading circle, or finding a movie that depicts the life of someone who is homeless (see background below).

Other Metaphorical Uses or Parallels

This book could also be used to talk about family norms and school expectations by showing how the behaviors that are exhibited might actually be acceptable in one place and not in another.

Illustrations

The illustrations are typical Dr. Seuss pictures and depict his various characters in different ways to tell the story.

Recommended Background Reading

Central Station, movie on homeless child in Brazil. Review at www .aspin.asu.edu/hpn/archives/Nov98/0355.html (retrieved March 1, 2004). *The Homeless Home Movie*. Review at www.2.bitstream.net/~mvisions (retrieved March 1, 2004).

K. Jackson, *Family Homelessness* (New York: Taylor & Francis, 2000); K. L. Lively and P. F. Kleine, *School as a Tool for Survival for Homeless Children* (New York: Taylor & Francis, 1996).

Insight into Action

Determine the ways in which teachers can become better educated about the needs of students who are homeless. Set up a checkpoint during the semester to ensure that there is follow-up to the decisions made by the group, whether to view a movie or read and discuss a book, or to volunteer at a center where homeless families stay.

ECONOMIC UNCERTAINTIES: ACTIVITY 3

Purpose

The purpose of this activity is to help teachers understand that even when children live in poverty, they can still find beauty in the world around them.

Materials

- Book: B. Collier, *Uptown* (New York: Holt, 2000). ISBN 0-8050-5721-8

Abstract of the Children's Book

This story is a child's view of all that is right with living in Harlem, a community that for many epitomizes danger and poverty. The boy tells the joys that exist in Harlem through music and the vibrancy of the community. A reader who can imitate a child of African American heritage will make this story richer.

Setting the Stage

1. Are there parts of your community where you are afraid to drive alone?
2. When was the last time you asked a child of poverty to describe the beauty in his or her life?

Notes on Reading the Book

Read the book with excitement, joy, and wonder as the child beholds the beauty of the world and the faith he has of the adults around him.

Discussion Questions

1. How much of what we expect regarding students' behavior is based on our own middle class expectations?
2. List three things you believe to be beautiful in the poorest section of the community.
3. With students, what aspects of our community can we identify as being uniquely ours and beautiful?

Facilitating the Discussion

1. In the first question it is important to help teachers realize that regardless of their own background, being in the teaching ranks puts them in the middle class, if not the upper middle class. This may have been by design or may be the result of planning. But the behaviors that allow one to succeed as a teacher may result in confusion about the behaviors that students of poverty bring to school. Discuss ways they can coexist.
2. Ask teachers to share their observations for question 2 and then collect their ideas and generate a list that can be shared among the faculty and staff.
3. Discuss ways that students can be engaged in finding beauty in their community, whether it is in the heart of a kind person on their street, a generous community member who gives time to help others, or music or art from those in the community.

Other Metaphorical Uses or Parallels

This book can also be used to discuss issues related to race, culture, and ethnicity.

Illustrations

The illustrations are bold and colorful and clearly reflect the images engendered by the descriptions of Harlem. Be sure to share them even if you pass the book around after the reading.

Recommended Background Reading

J. Metzger, *Kids Count on Families: A Special Report on the State of Our Families* (1995). Report for Arkansas Advocates for Children and Families. ERIC Document ED 422084.

Insight into Action

Share the insights that teachers have about different ways that beauty can be defined in a community and how it can transcend the physical environment. Post the results of the project on your website.

ECONOMIC UNCERTAINTIES: ACTIVITY 4

Purpose

The purpose of this activity is to explore the dignity that accompanies all work and to help teachers understand the complex emotions that accompany parental underemployment, the inability to provide for one's family, and the burdens that children bear in such circumstances.

Materials

- Book: E. Bartone, *Peppe the Lamplighter* (New York: Mulberry, 1993). ISBN: 0-688-15469-7

Abstract of the Children's Book

An immigrant family struggles for survival in New York City at a time "when there was no electricity and the streetlamps in Little Italy had to be lit by hand." In order to help his family, young Peppe looks for work. He is thrilled when he gets a job as a lamplighter; his father, however, is displeased, as he envisions more for his son than simply working on the street. When a young sister disappears, Peppe's father comes to appreciate the efforts and value of Peppe's work and Peppe again gathers strength from his hopes and dreams.

Setting the Stage

Note: The following questions should be given to participants one question at a time. Let them write their response to the first question before reading (or distributing) the second question.

1. What was the first paying job you ever held?
2. Why do you work now?
3. Why do you work in education?
4. Explain your likely reaction if you were to once again hold the job you described in response to the first question.

Notes on Reading the Book

This children's book is written for older children; the text is somewhat long and complex. The best reader for this selection is someone who can read clearly and somewhat quickly. It is also imperative that the reader have the ability to pronounce a series of Italian first names without stumbling; practice makes perfect.

Discussion Questions

1. What rewards did you garner, beyond a paycheck, from your first paying job? What did you learn from that experience? How did it shape you? What feedback did you get from your parents and/or your community about that job?

2. How do the benefits (tangible and intangible) of your current job compare with those of your earliest experience? What has changed? What remains the same?
3. Would you work if you didn't have to? Why or why not?
4. What do you suspect the home life is like for students in your school who have a parent who is unemployed or under-employed? How is that familial experience likely to shape their behavior and feelings in—and about—school and their likely future?
5. What are the psychological effects of chronic unemployment or underemployment? What lessons do children in such families learn, particularly in light of the message that we give students that they can do or be anything?
6. Based on their conduct in your class, what do you suspect certain students have learned about work, based on their experiences in their family and community?

Facilitating the Discussion

Many American families, no matter what their socioeconomic status, educational level, or profession, have experienced unemployment or underemployment in recent years. Akin to the Great Depression, many families are coping with a type and duration of economic uncertainty that few expected. It is quite likely that some participants will have firsthand experience with this type of trauma. Reactions may run the gamut from indifference to anger to reflective sadness. Keep the focus on how our own experiences can shape those of the students we teach, and how our understanding of their familial difficulties can shape their school experiences and academic success.

We often remind students that education is key to their eventual success, not only developmentally, but also in terms of future economic security. How do we reconcile the message, "To get a good job, get a good education," with economic realities, as well as the contradictory messages students might hear at home? How do we reconcile the seemingly paradoxical statements of "Be all you can be" with "All work is honorable if it's done well"?

Other Metaphorical Uses or Parallels

This story could be used to generate discussions about the power of family relationships, family norms based on culture and ethnicity, historical discussions about city tenement life, or "family values."

Illustrations

Ted Lewin earned a Caldecott Honor for his illustrations. The dark tones and prevalence of grays and blacks convey the ominous tone of much of this book. The pictures, however, similarly communicate the underlying optimism and hope to which Peppe resolutely clings.

Recommended Background Reading

B. Ehrenreich, *Nickled and Dimed: On (Not) Getting By in America* (New York: Holt, 2002).

Insight into Action

The overriding message of this text is that all work is honorable and valuable. What comments are made in your school, or in your classroom, that make light of or minimize the importance of certain jobs or categories of jobs? Are some classroom questions or discussions about work, while seemingly benign on the surface, actually loaded for students? At the high school level, are students made fun of if they work in the fast food industry? Are students consciously or subconsciously dissuaded from investigating particular occupations (i.e., "With teeth like that, you're not good-looking enough to go into broadcasting," or "You're too smart to just be a teacher")? Are some students ridiculed for working in particular occupations? Is anything done in your school community to mitigate such comments and attitudes? At the elementary level, what values and prejudices might be conveyed to students about the meaning of certain types of work? What type of occupations are routinely promoted, and why? Who are the occupational role models who visit your school? What messages do such visits convey to students about their own futures and potential, and about the contributions made by students' parents? Does our school's overriding message honor or dishonor "menial" work? Continue the discussion generated by this activity on your school's discussion board, or at a subsequent professional development session, if interest warrants it.

ECONOMIC UNCERTAINTIES: ACTIVITY 5

Purpose

The purpose of this activity is to help teachers understand, beyond the loss of shelter, the myriad consequences and losses that accompany homelessness.

Materials

- Book: A. Mazer, *The Salamander Room* (New York: Dragonfly, 1991). ISBN 0-679-86187-4

Abstract of the Children's Book

A young boy finds a salamander in the woods and takes him home to be his pet. Through a series of probing questions, the boy explains everything he will do to create a comfortable and adequate home for his salamander, in effect turning his own bedroom into a forest.

Setting the Stage

1. Make a list of all of the things you would lose or miss if you were to suddenly become homeless.
2. Next, prioritize your list from "the number one thing that I would most miss or hate to lose," to the item that would be the easiest to do without. (In other words, number each item from 1 on down in priority order.)

Notes on Reading the Book

This is a wonderfully short yet powerful book. In this text, a dialogue occurs between a mother and her young son. As such, the book could be read as a conversation using male and female voices; the male voice conveys the enthusiasm and optimism of youth, the female voice echoes the forethought and insight of an adult.

Discussion Questions

Note: Divide participants into small groups of five to seven. Compare and contrast your lists. What commonalities do your lists have? In what ways are they different?

1. As you compared and contrasted your lists, were any of the items that emerged emotional or imperceptible things, such as loss of security, loss of the physical presence of familiar people, loss of self-esteem or self-worth, or the stress of having to move?
2. Which physical things were ranked as important? What symbolic or emotional value do those tangible things hold? What meaning or importance might children attach to such things?
3. Was it hard for you, either individually or as a group, to take this exercise seriously because of the far-fetched nature of the questions? Is it difficult for you to imagine yourself ever being homeless? Why?

Facilitating the Discussion

1. As you review the lists and the priorities assigned to various items, note the commonalities of lists. Did pragmatic, concrete losses dominate? Why or why not?
2. Ask representatives from each group to report on both the content and affect of their discussions. (If the group is large, you may be able to hear from only some groups, in the interest of time and brevity.) Were group members cognizant of the emotional weight of some of these losses?
3. If some participants had a hard time taking this exercise as seriously as it is intended, or if some individuals seemed reluctant to participate, what meaning do you attribute to such behavior? Do you suspect some of us know too little (or too much) about the power of homelessness?
4. If the situation and climate seem conducive, and if the group is cohesive, you might probe about teachers' personal experiences with

homelessness or a threat of homelessness. It's perfectly okay to broach this topic, as long as you recognize that although homelessness is never the fault of children, some of us, even as adults, are reluctant or outright refuse to share such histories with professional peers.

5. Emphasize that although most participants could readily identify with tangible losses, the accompanying emotional losses are far harder to remediate than are the disappearance of concrete things we often associate with homelessness.

Other Metaphorical Uses or Parallels

This book is a lovely story about caretaking and friendship. It could be used to demonstrate the selflessness that accompanies all great gifts, the subjugation of self for the needs of others, or the complexity of simple survival.

Illustrations

Pay particular attention to the transformation of Brian's room from a typical boy's bedroom to an extension of the forest. The illustrations by Steve Johnson and Lou Fancher capture the magic and mystery of the physical metamorphosis beautifully. Do not neglect the very last page, which contains no text but simply the salamander and the boy sleeping next to each other in their respective beds.

Recommended Background Reading

J. Kozol, *Savage Inequalities: Children in America's Schools* (New York: HarperCollins, 1992); Kozol, *Rachel and Her Children: Homeless Families in America* (New York: Fawcett, 1989).

Insight into Action

In addition to having lists of services that can assist families that are homeless in acquiring the concrete necessities of survival, as a school community, try to provide for some of the intangible needs of such families. For example, can transportation be provided to enable such families to attend community events? Are Welcome Wagon activities available to acquaint such families to resources, services, and events, such as local libraries?

For individual teachers: If you have a student who is currently homeless and likely to move from your school or district once more stable housing is found, make for that student a scrapbook or folder with pictures of yourself and your students, a list of that student's favorite classroom activities, and a note about the gifts that you recognize the student brought to your classroom. For children who are experiencing homelessness, permanence and a sense of stability are elusive. Change is constant. By giving your student a concrete record of their time with you, you are providing not only a record of time spent in one place but an element of memory in an otherwise chaotic and fragmented world.

5

EVALUATION

EVALUATING AND REFINING THESE
PROFESSIONAL DEVELOPMENT ACTIVITIES

The purpose of this chapter is to help instructional leaders evaluate the effectiveness of the professional development activities provided in this handbook. Instructional leaders will also be able to determine ways to refine the process for use in their environments and consider ways to monitor the Insight into Action for their schools.

The Need for Evaluation

A perusal of the preceding chapters elicits the inevitable conclusion that professional development programs, whether those built on the activities outlined in this handbook or inspired by other sources, demand a sizable commitment of energy, time, and resources. Was the effort worth it? Did the program, as delivered, result in the desired outcomes? If so, how do you know?

A professional development program that is worth doing is worth evaluating. Although the authors have tested the strategies recommended herein, every school and every context is different. Assumptions about a learning community's needs, as well as the initiatives that flow from such assumptions, must be assessed. Did the program address a real need? Were program participants receptive to the activities and the message? A perceptive administrator can ascertain a faculty's response by simply observing reactions and interactions following the program. It is our assertion, however, that truly successful professional development programs result not simply in satisfaction immediately following the presentation or activity, but they continue to inform and improve educational practice in the days and weeks that follow. Thus, our aim in proposing an evaluation strategy is to encourage program planners and presenters to take the long view, that is, to recognize that successful professional development programs are, or should be, developmental in nature. Meaningful professional development programs nurture ongoing dialogue and continue to shape what happens in the classroom long after the microphone and materials have been stowed away. If that is the aim, what kind of evaluation strategy can capture such longitudinal effects?

Criteria for Successful Evaluation in the Context of Professional Development

Traditional evaluation strategies tended to focus on measurement and/or description (Guba and Lincoln 1989). While such methods served early efforts well, the complexity of current demands for accountability demand a more comprehensive and utilitarian approach. Measuring that which can be measured ("on a scale of 1 to 4, rate your satisfaction with this professional development program") or describing perceived strengths and weaknesses of a program (whether from an administrator's or teacher's perspective, whether formative or summative) have a place. Judgment, too, is an oft-requested goal of program evaluation: Is this program or strategy worth repeating? However, given the developmental nature of professional development, all of the three commonly used evaluation strategies (measurement, description, and judgment) are likely to deliver the types of information and insight that will allow program participants to continue their professional development long after the program has been completed. The type of evaluation strategy proposed for these activities demands ownership of the program *and* the evaluation by participants. Also necessary is authenticity in documenting the immediate *and* ongoing effects of the program. And best practice demands an examination of how, if at all, the program effects student learning and success. Surely this is a tall order, given the limited time and resources of most school-based personnel.

Looking for a Strategy That Works

Based on more than five years of field testing the professional development strategies and programs outlined here, we know that in both primary and secondary schools teachers respond favorably to both the form and content of these activities. But how will the unique individuals in your specific learning community respond to, and grow from, the information and inspiration that flows from these activities? All schools are unique; as a complex organization, a school's culture reflects the particular constellation of individuals that define and shape the community. Although the programs themselves appear quite rigid, the unveiling of interpretations, based on individual values, will dramatically shape what the final product looks like. Although the form is prescribed, the outcomes vary widely in terms of how professionals take, use, and recycle their new insights. Similarly, the translation of Insight to Action plays out differently in each unique context. Hence, to bolster the utility of the program over time, to ascertain the degree to which these professional development activities positively affect professional practice, and in order to design future professional development agendas, program evaluation is essential.

Given the developmental nature of our approach, common assumptions regarding the primary mission of evaluation (i.e., measurement, description, or judgment) are not as critical in this process as that of a site-based evaluation program built upon the standards promulgated by the Joint Committee on Standards in Education Evaluation (i.e., utility, feasibility, propriety, and accuracy). While all the standards (Guskey 1999) should be considered on the part of the administrator supporting the programs, the guidelines for best practice are summarized below, and the evaluation strategy is described and explained. A number of assumptions, however, guide our recommended approach to evaluation. These assumptions address both commonly accepted standards of best practice in the evaluation of educational programs (generally) and professional development programs (specifically) as well as the authors' values and hopes for the desired outcome that propels us through this work.

Evaluation of professional development programs must be doable within the context of the school. By doable, we mean the evaluation is conservative of time and resources, easy to implement, and generates data that all stakeholders can understand and use. Such criteria speak to the demand for feasibility; if an evaluation strategy lacks practicality, it cannot, and will not, be embraced by a school community, the audience it is meant to inform and serve. Underlining this assumption is that program evaluation isn't something that is done to a program, but is rather an essential and natural outgrowth of an educational initiative rooted in a learning community. As such, the program itself, and its subsequent evaluation, belongs to program participants. The goal, after all, is improvement of professional practice. Any evaluation strategy, if it is truly useful to the organization, must examine the extent to which program outcomes affect changes in teacher behavior and performance, and thus improves student learning and success. The evaluation must have utility.

Because professional development should be a developmental process for educators, the best assessments center on the evolution of professional practice. Ownership of the "product" is the educator's; professional development is not something "done to" school staff, but is, when effective, a component of personal, as well as professional, growth. This speaks to standards of propriety; professional development programs and their assessment are not neutral activities. The success of both is deeply dependent on teacher commitment, motivation, and professionalism. As such, they are value dependent, value loaded, and value centered.

Building on these assumptions, one-shot paper-and-pencil surveys cannot capture the desired effects envisioned through these programs. Often, professional development activities plant seeds that sprout and flower over time. The evaluation strategy we recommend is thus rooted in a longitudinal perspective in order to provide accuracy. Furthermore, the intentions of the professional development activity are to bring about a change in individual behavior and positive movement of a learning community as a whole. When effective, these programs are synergistic, as they affect the developing "learning culture" of the educational environment. Teachers, after all, shape and are shaped by each other. This evaluation strategy capitalizes on this interdependence. Successful schools are those in which all staff members function as a team. The evaluation strategy we propose nurtures both the development of teamwork and the emergence of leadership.

While very technical program evaluations are desirable and encouraged, the ongoing nature of these activities and the opportunity for dialogue among professionals suggests that we identify an evaluation agenda. What can a school staff do that is easy, effective, longitudinal, and developmental, as well as capable of accurately capturing where a community of educators is and where they need to go? It seems a tall order, and indeed it is. Certainly, the one-shot, one-page, one-correct response, and one-dimensional, or even one-minute assessment, won't do. What will?

Using Technology for Program Assessment

Following is a strategy to capture participants' feedback and insights from the program and to provide a forum for sharing ideas and insights on the designated professional development topic. The strategy demands an ongoing dialogue on the topic, a dialogue that can

1. Garner feedback on format as well as content
2. Point to necessary next steps
3. Allow participants to revise their insights and practices over time to further the learning process for peers
4. Assess the impact of the program on student learning

An ideal tool to meet these demands and address such concerns is the school's computer system, specifically the use of discussion boards (or lists) hosted on the school or school district's computer system. A computerized discussion list, as an evaluative tool, can provide information that is

1. Accessible anytime, therefore free of time frame constraints
2. Authentic, as posted content is not prescribed or restricted

3. New, with related and relevant information or insights able to be shared even long after the initial professional development program is over
4. Free flowing between teachers and staff
5. A vehicle for sharing information without a face-to-face staff meeting
6. A vehicle to nurture the development of computer skills for the technically challenged
7. Controllable by the teachers rather than an administrator, thus fostering the development of new leadership
8. Low cost and time efficient
9. Posted and therefore open to challenge and discussion, thus ensuring that the validity and reliability of information is constantly monitored
10. Capable of identifying pertinent next steps, so that relevant activities can be developed
11. Deemed worthy of a professional development activity and thus may emerge and be readily identified
12. A basis for authentic assessment
13. A tool for the ongoing creation and maintenance of a learning community, as sources, references, and valuable materials may be easily shared via links or attachments

SUMMARY ON USE OF DISCUSSION BOARDS

While the more standard and identified forms of professional development evaluation should be part of any ongoing staff development, the purpose in describing the advantages to online discussion boards is to encourage administrators and facilitators to consider that everyone in education has to "work smarter" and utilize the time gain that technology allows us. Additionally, an advantage of technology is that those who may be reluctant to speak in a group may feel more comfortable posting to a discussion board. Likewise, the record of discussion provides a basis for ongoing evaluation and future professional development activities.

Drawbacks of Using a Discussion List for Evaluative Purposes

The benefits of discussion lists, such as cost, authenticity, ease, and richness, are counterbalanced by potential drawbacks. While not insurmountable, the following cautions are offered to help program planners anticipate limitations and concerns of a computerized system for program assessment.

1. Technophobes—teach 'em
2. System failure—back it up
3. Questions of anonymity—judgment call
4. Site monitor—identify the most knowledgeable
5. Divisiveness rather than synergy—rely on monitor (conflict becomes grist for the mill)
6. Lurkers—restrict access
7. Bad behavior—identify expectations upfront
8. Lack of participation or interest—ascertain reason: Fear? Reluctance? Topic is not a priority?
9. Fear of sensitive material falling into the wrong hands

EVALUATION THE OLD-FASHIONED WAY

There can certainly be a time and place for quick feedback or a more long-term evaluation of any professional development. With many years of practice with paper-and-pencil surveys, many educators find them a more comfortable way to respond. Overall, we suggest that the use of paper-and-pencil feedback should be for short-term assessment of issues and concerns; use a more long-term approach, such as computer-based feedback, to monitor the effectiveness of the professional development activities.

FREQUENTLY ASKED QUESTIONS ON DISCUSSION BOARDS

How long should a discussion list stay active? As long as someone is able to monitor the site and the dialogue is continuous, it will be important to maintain it. If after ten to fourteen days no one is responding, then it is time to garner the information gathered on the discussion board and analyze it for direction and assessment of the effects of the activities.

Should anonymous posts be allowed or welcomed? Anonymous postings will be largely dependent on the purpose of the discussion board and an assessment of who can access it. If you are confident that the discussion board is limited to program participants, then there will certainly be topics that you will want to consider for anonymous postings. When any discussion board is used, participants should be informed upfront as to the anonymity (or not) of the postings.

What if the site's discussion gets off-task? The purpose for appointing a monitor for the discussion board is to ensure that the discussion remains focused on the topic and that any additional issues that are raised are brought to the attention of the administrator for future opportunities to discuss.

Can we still do a simple paper-and-pencil survey to see if participants liked the program? Of course there is a place for this type of survey. It is quick and can provide immediate feedback on things like presentation style, length of activities, meaningfulness, and so on. However, the use of a discussion board to continue the dialogue and encourage reflective practice will have more long-term effects.

How long should the site remain active? In a school where decisions are driven by healthy dialogue among professionals, a site that allows discussion based on professional development activities, as well as a forum for raising new issues, is a healthy tool and should probably be ongoing.

The evaluation information provided for this handbook is not intended to be a treatise on evaluation or a comprehensive guide to program evaluation. You are encouraged to be familiar with professional development program standards (Guskey 1999) and use them as appropriate in any and all professional development programs.

EPILOGUE

CHILDREN'S LITERATURE AS PARABLE

This volume grew out of Jacque's work in providing professional development for schools, and her idea to incorporate the same strategies for use in teaching graduate courses in the supervision of instruction. Both professional development efforts in schools and the preservice program in which we teach are based on developing administrative and teaching skills in the adults responsible for what goes on in our schools. At its heart, this is a deeply moral enterprise. This quiet knowledge has spurred us to choose the topics we've included here, and has pushed us to complete this volume.

In a sense, we are just beginning—beginning to fully understand the dynamics of professional development (which is simply lifelong learning in another guise), beginning to appreciate the required energy and commitment that accompanies administrative efforts to provide meaningful and relevant professional development on a routine basis, and beginning to understand the complexities of organizational change and resistance to change. We have, in a sense, come full circle. From our first conversations about professional development we understood that the real work is in changing how teachers think about the work they do, not simply with students but also with students' parents and each other.

We had fun finding books to address topics central to the business of schools, teaching, and learning, which are addressed in this book's companion volume. We looked for school-related topics first, but as we scoured the shelves of Barnes and Noble for children's books that we could use in this project, a subtle but startling realization dawned on us: many of the books for which we had the greatest resonance and affection were volumes that spoke to us of moral purpose, of our shared humanity, of something about the human condition that enveloped schools and schooling but somehow superseded the narrow confines of the educational establishment.

Many of the children's books we use here have a moral heart. They are about what it means to share, to be part of a family and community, how good things come to those who persevere, how justice can prevail even in the most difficult circumstances. It may be somewhat surprising to some of you that these themes are embedded in so many children's books. But why is that surprising? Don't we try to instill such values in children when they are young? Don't we want our own children, and the children and young people we teach, to be, above all else, decent humans? I think most of us, while we were reading *Where the Wild Things Are* or *Make Way for Ducklings* to our own children, didn't dwell much on the underlying messages inherent in such simple stories. We were preaching, though, via these innocent children's books, that the world is really a safe place, that children are precious beyond words, that the world is beautiful, awesome (in its true sense: full of awe), and wonderful (in its true sense, full of wonder). Ah, but do we really believe such things?

Maybe children's books are parables—stories that seek to impart a moral lesson, divulge a higher purpose. Like all good literature, there is a dark thread that weaves, sometimes undetected, through these stories. They are not all light and easy, uncomplicated and innocent. The stories that are richest, for our purposes, are those that acknowledge the struggle to overcome the obstacles, both large and small, that greet all of us on our traipse through life. *Hey, Get Off Our Train, Satchel Paige, McDuff Moves In*, and *Stone Soup*, among many more, share the common characteristic of divulging human cruelty. Ultimately, however, kindness trumps indifference, and ingenuity, altruism, and a taste for justice override pessimism and despair.

As authors and as teachers, we are optimists at heart. We couldn't continue to do what we do if we didn't think our efforts could somehow make a difference in the lives of teachers and students. We see the political callousness toward education, and we hear and read the conservative pundits who assign blame where it is least deserved: on the heads and shoulders of children and young people. Schools don't need more money, they assert, choosing to note the increases in education funding. What too many don't see, and what those of us intimately acquainted with schools do, is that it's *not* about money but rather what money can buy.

Yes, we are all waiting for the education messiah to come, but it looks like she's not about to arrive anytime soon. In the interim, we use what we have: our intellect, our energies, our creativity, and our time to make a difference in the lives of students everywhere. This is a deeply moral enterprise, for it is about the development and unleashing of human potential trapped, too often, in circumstances that no one inside of a school can control. In the interim, we continue to read books—children's and adults'—for keys to the kingdom, for insights into the human heart, and for connections that we can make to improve *schools and schooling* as we learn to *cope in a changing world*. To ignore the demands is to fail not simply as educators but as human beings. We all have to be somewhere doing something, so we might as well be somewhere doing something that matters. For the two of us, it is scratching beneath the pastel-patterned surfaces of children's literature, engaging in critical dialogue with our students, and forging connections between what teachers know, believe, and feel and the students they see daily. It is a moral enterprise, a work steeped in humane values, aimed at not simply the intellect but the human heart.

APPENDIX A: OPINION POLL ON PARENTAL BEHAVIORS

For each of the behaviors or situations described below, please note if the parental behavior that is described is, *in your opinion*,

A. Abuse
B. Neglect
C. "Bad parenting"
D. Although not good parenting, it's sometimes a necessary behavior
E. A legitimate type of child rearing; a parental prerogative

_____1. A parent "spanks" a ten-year-old boy's naked bottom with a leather belt.

_____2. A second grade child accompanies a parent to Wal-Mart at 2:00 A.M. on a school night to purchase groceries.

_____3. A child is sent to school with a crust of bread for lunch.

_____4. A fourth grade child wears the same articles of clothing to school every day for two weeks, and it is painfully clear that the clothes have not been laundered.

_____5. A parent calls a first grader a stupid idiot for forgetting her lunch at home.

_____6. A fifth grade girl wears a lace bra and thong underwear to school underneath a short skirt and crop top. She reports that her father bought the undergarments for her and encourages her to wear them.

_____7. A third grade child is left on the front steps of the school building at 5:45 A.M., as his mother has to report for work at 6:00 A.M. at a fast food establishment.

_____8. A sixth grade child complains of a toothache and reports that he has never seen a dentist. The school nurse examines his teeth; they are severely decayed.

_____9. A twelve-year-old girl accompanies her mother and father to an R-rated movie.

_____10. A seven-year-old boy accompanies his father to an R-rated movie.

_____11. A twelve-year-old girl reports that her parents refuse to buy her, or give her money for, sanitary napkins.

_____12. An eight-year-old boy baby-sits for his five-year-old sister while his mother and grandmother play bingo from 6:00 to 10:00 P.M. on a school night.

_____13. A stepfather "spanks" a twelve-year-old girl's naked bottom with a leather belt.

_____14. A second grade boy comes to school with pants that are so big, they keep falling down. He has no underpants underneath.

_____15. Routinely, two brothers, in kindergarten and first grade, have the sole responsibility to get themselves up, get ready for school, and go out to meet the bus while their parents "sleep it off."

_____16. Middle school children are allowed to watch X-rated videos at home.

_____17. Children ages nine, eleven, and fifteen are given a glass of wine with their dinner to celebrate their dad's promotion at work.

_____18. A high school girl is slapped, hard, across the face by her father for uttering an obscenity.

_____19. A first grade child is locked in the family's bathroom overnight for wetting the bed.

_____20. A child reports on Monday morning that she didn't have much to eat all weekend, as her mother needed what little cash they had to buy lottery tickets.

APPENDIX B: PROFESSIONAL DEVELOPMENT ACTIVITY: DIVERSITY

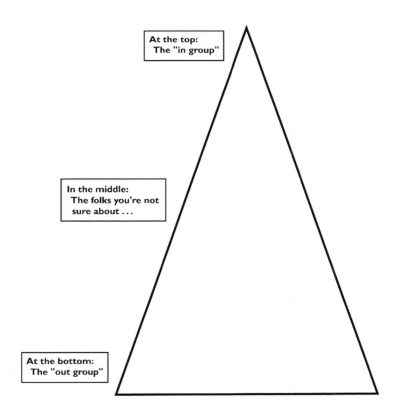

At the top:
The "in group"

In the middle:
The folks you're not
sure about . . .

At the bottom:
The "out group"

APPENDIX C: SAMPLE OUTLINE FOR CREATING YOUR OWN ACTIVITIES

Topic:
Purpose:

Materials:
   Book:
   ISBN
   Materials:

Abstract of the children's book:

Setting the stage:
1.
2.
3.

Notes on reading the book:

Discussion questions:
1.
2.
3.

Facilitating the discussion:
1.
2.
3.

Other metaphorical uses or parallels:

Illustrations:

Recommended background reading:

Insight into action:

SELECTED CHILDREN'S LITERATURE

Ackermann, A., and Ackermann, A. 2001. *Our Mom Has Cancer.* Atlanta: American Cancer Society.

Allsburg, C. V. 1987. *The Z Was Zapped.* Boston: Houghton Mifflin.

Altman, L. J. 2002. *Singing with Momma Lou.* New York: Lee & Low.

Barnwell, Y. M. 1998. *No Mirrors in My Nana's House.* Orlando, FL: Harcourt Brace.

Bartone, E. 1993. *Peppe the Lamplighter.* New York: Mulberry.

Bostrom, K. L. 1998. *What Is God Like?* Wheaton, IL: Tyndale.

Briers, E. 2003. *Little Duck Lost.* New York: Dutton Children's Books.

Bruchac, J. 1998. *The First Strawberries.* New York: Puffin.

Bunting, E. 1994. *Smoky Night.* Orlando, FL: Harcourt Brace.

Burningham, J. 1994. *Hey! Get Off Our Train.* New York: Crown Books for Young Readers.

Cline-Ransome, L. 2000. *Satchel Paige.* New York: Simon & Schuster Books for Young Readers.

Cogdill, M. 2002. *Cracker the Crab and the Sideways Afternoon.* Simpsonville, SC: Two Bear.

Collier, B. 2000. *Uptown.* New York: Holt.

Eastman, P. D. 1988. *Are You My Mother? ¿Eres tu mi mama?* New York: Random House.

Feelings, T. 1993. *Soul Looks Back in Wonder.* New York: Dial.

Feiffer, J. 2002. *The House across the Street.* New York: Michael di Capua/Hyperion Books for Children.

Fierstein, H. 2002. *The Sissy Duckling.* New York: Simon & Schuster Books for Young Readers.

Fleischman, P. 2003. *The Animal Hedge.* Cambridge, MA: Candlewick.

Hankes, K. 2000. *Chrysanthemum.* New York: Green Willow.

Hanson, W. 1997. *The Next Place.* Minneapolis: Waldman.

Hawkins, C., and Hawkins, J. 2004. *Fairytale News.* Cambridge, MA: Candlewick.

Heide, F. P., and Gilliland, J. H. 1990. *The Day of Ahmed's Secret.* New York: Lothrop, Lee & Shepard.

Jackson, E. 2002. *Sometimes Bad Things Happen.* Brookfield, CT: Millbrook.

Johnson, A. 2004. *Just Like Josh Gibson.* New York: Simon & Schuster Books for Young Readers.

Jordan, D., and Jordan, R. M. 2000. *Salt in His Shoes.* New York: Simon & Schuster.

Keido, I. 2003. *The Butterfly's Dream.* Boston: Tuttle.

Kubler-Ross, Elisabeth. 1997. *On Death and Dying.* New York: Scribner.

Lansky, V. 1998. *It's Not Your Fault, Koko Bear.* Minnetonka, MN: Book Peddlers.

Lasne, J. 1994. *The Red Ribbon.* Greenville, SC: Woofgang Brand Development.

Lewis, R. 2000. *I Love You Like Crazy Cakes.* Boston: Little, Brown.

Lithgow, J. 2000. *The Remarkable Farkle McBride.* New York: Simon & Schuster Books for Young Readers.

Livingston, I. 2003. *Finklehopper Frog.* Berkeley: CA: Tricycle.

McCain, B. C. 2001. *Nobody Knew What to Do: A Story about Bullying.* Morton Grove, IL: Albert Whitman.

McGough, R. 2002. *Moonthief.* New York: Houghton Mifflin.

McKissack, P. C. 2000. *The Honest-to-Goodness Truth.* New York: Simon & Schuster Children's Division.

McPhail, D. 1999. *Mole Music.* New York: Holt.

Mazer, A. 1991. *The Salamander Room.* New York: Dragonfly.

Miller, J. H., and Miller, T. 1994. *The Mighty Hugo Comes to Town.* New York: Jereleen H. Miller.

Munsch, R. N. 1985. *The Paperbag Princess.* Ontario, Canada: Annick.

Muth, J. J. 2002. *The Three Questions.* New York: Scholastic.

———. 2003. *Stone Soup.* New York: Scholastic.

Myers, C. 2000. *Wings.* New York: Scholastic.

Numeroff, L. 1996. *Why a Disguise?* New York: Simon & Schuster Books for Young Readers.

Peterseil, Y. 1999. *Princess Alopecia.* New York: Pitspopany.

Polacco, P. 2001. *Mr. Lincoln's Way.* New York: Philomel.

Rabe, T. 2003. *The Fish's Tale.* New York: Random House.

Riley, L. 1997. *Mouse Mess.* New York: Scholastic.

Ringgold, F. 1991. *Tar Beach.* New York: Crown.

Rogers, F. 1998. *Let's Talk about It: Adoption.* New York: Putnam & Grosset.

Sander, M. D., and Sillers, T. 2003. *I Hope You Dance!* Nashville, TN: Rutledge Hill.

Sasso, S. E. 1994. *In God's Name.* Woodstock, VT: Jewish Lights.

Schwiebert, P., and DeKlyen, C. 1999. *Tear Soup: A Recipe for Healing after Loss.* Portland: Grief Watch.

Scieszka, J. 1989. *The True Story of the Three Little Pigs.* New York: Viking.

Scott, A. H. 1992. *On Mother's Lap.* New York: Clarion.

Seskin, S., and Shamblin, A. 2002. *Don't Laugh at Me.* Berkeley, CA: Ten Speed.

Shannon, D. 2000. *The Rain Come Down.* New York: Blue Sky.

Shriver, M. 2001. *What's Wrong with Timmy?* New York: Warner Books/Little, Brown.

Silverstein, S. 1981. *The Missing Piece Meets the Big O.* New York: Harper-Collins.

Steig, W. 1990. *Doctor De Soto.* New York: Farrar, Straus & Giroux.

Stevens, J. 1995. *Tops and Bottoms.* New York: Scholastic.

Steward, S. 1997. *The Gardener.* New York: Sunbursts/Farrar Strauss Giroux. A Caldecott Honor Book.

Taback, S. 1998. *Joseph Had a Little Overcoat.* New York: Penguin.

Tarpley, N. A. 1998. *I Love My Hair.* Boston: Megan Tingley.

Thaler, M. 1997. *The Librarian from the Black Lagoon.* New York: Scholastic.

Thurber, J. 1971. *Many Moons.* Orlando, FL: Harcourt Brace.

Varley, S. 1984. *Badger's Parting Gifts.* New York: Mulberry.

Vigna, J. 1988. *I Wish Daddy Didn't Drink So Much.* Morton Grove, IL: Albert Whitman.

Viorst, J. 1995. *Alexander, Who's Not (Do You Hear Me? I Mean It!) Going to Move.* New York: Scholastic.

Waber, B. 2002. *Courage.* Boston: Houghton Mifflin.

Wachter, O. 2002. *No More Secrets for Me: Sexual Abuse Is a Secret No Child Should Have to Keep.* Rev. ed. Boston: Little, Brown.

Well, S., and Jeffers, S. 1997. *McDuff Moves In.* New York: Hyperion Books for Children.

Whybrow, I. 1999. *Sammy and the Dinosaurs.* New York: Scholastic.

Wilson, K. 2004. *Hilda Must Be Dancing.* New York: Simon & Schuster Children's Publishing Division.

Wong, J. S. 2002. *Apple Pie Fourth of July*. New York: Harcourt.

Wynn, M. 1993. *The Eagles Who Thought They Were Chickens*. Marietta, GA: Rising Sun.

Yin. 2001. *Coolies*. New York: Philomel.

Young, E. 1992. *Seven Blind Mice*. New York: Philomel.

Young-Robinson, C. 2001. *Isra the Butterfly Gets Caught for Show and Tell*. Columbia, SC: Yoroson.

RECOMMENDED READINGS

Abuse and neglect information. www.indianchild.com/child_abuse.htm.

Abuse and neglect materials. www.mental-health-matters.com.

Affectional and sexual orientation study guides made available by the Human Rights Education Association. www.hrea.org/learn/guides/lgbt.html.

Al-Anon Family Group Headquarters, Inc., P.O. Box 862, Midtown Station, New York, NY 10018 (212-302-7240).

Alzheimer's Association website. www.alz.org.

Alzheimer's Disease Core Center (ADCC) website. www.brain.nwu.edu/core/index.htm.

Alzheimer's Disease Education and Referral (ADEAR) Center website. www.alzheimers.org.

American Psychiatric Association. 2004. "Let's Talk Facts about . . . Substance Abuse and Addiction." www.psych.org/public_info/substance.cfm.

American Psychological Association. 1997. "Cartoons Still Stereotype Gender Roles." APA news release.

Awareness of Chronic Health Conditions: What the Teacher Needs to Know. 1995. ERIC Document ED415602.

Banks, J. 1995. "The Historical Reconstruction of Knowledge about Race: Implications for Transformative Teaching." *Educational Researcher* 24, no. 2: 15–25.

Banks, J. A. 1994. "On Educating for Diversity: A Conversation with James A. Burke." *Educational Leadership* 51, no. 8: 21–31.

Barnwell, Y. M. 1998. *No Mirrors in My Nana's House*. Orlando, FL: Harcourt Brace.

Beyer, L. E., ed. 1996. *Creating Democratic Classrooms: The Struggle to Integrate Theory and Practice*. New York: Teachers College Press.

Biddle, B. J., and Berliner, D. C. 2002. "Unequal School Funding in the United States." *Educational Leadership* 59, no. 8: 48–59.

Block, M. E. 1995. "Americans with Disabilities Act: Its Impact on Youth Sports." *Journal of Physical Education, Recreation, and Dance* 66, no. 1: 28–33.

Bruder, I. 1992. "Multicultural Education: Responding to the Demographics of Change." *Electronic Learning* 12, no. 2: 20–26.

Bullard, H. R. 2004. "Ensure the Successful Inclusion of a Child with Asperger Syndrome in the General Education Classroom." *Intervention in School and Clinic* 39, no. 3: 176.

Byrnes, D. 2000. "Talking with Children about Loss." *Childhood Education* 77, no. 2: 112.

Canada, J. 2000. "Raising Better Boys." *Educational Leadership* 59, no. 6: 14–17.

Cancer materials. www.cancer.org.

Carlin, D. R. 1996. "Teaching Values in School." *Commonweal* 123, no. 3: 7.

Central Station, review, a movie about a homeless child in Brazil. www.sony pictures.com/classics/Centralstation/frames.html (retrieved March 1, 2004).

Character education website. www.charactercounts.org.

Children's Living Arrangements and Characteristics: March 2002. Washington, D.C.: Census Bureau. www.census.gov/prod/2003pubs/p20-547.pdf.

"Children and Divorce: Helping Your Children Cope." www.bcm.tmc.edu/we_ care/divorce.htm.

Children of Alcoholics Foundation, Inc., 555 Madison Ave., 4th floor, New York, NY 10022 (212-754-0656).

Choi, Y. 2001. *The Name Jar*. New York: Random House Children's Books.

Cline-Ransome, L. 2000. *Satchel Paige*. New York: Simon & Schuster Books for Young Readers.

Colgrove, M., Bloomfield, H. H., and McWilliams, P. 1995. *How to Survive the Loss of a Love*. New York: Prelude.

Compas, B. E., and Boyer, M. C. 2001. "Coping and Attention: Implications for Child Health and Pediatric Conditions." *Journal of Developmental and Behavioral Pediatrics* 22, no. 5: 323–34.

Crow, S. M., and Hartman, S. J. 2003. "Responding to Threats of Workplace Violence: The Effects of Culture and Moral Panic." *Health Care Manager* 22, no. 4: 340–49.

Damon, W. 1992. "Teaching Values in School Promotes Understanding and Good Citizenship." *Brown University Child and Adolescent Behavior Letter* 8, no. 10: 3.

Davis, S., Hunt, R., and Jenkins, G. 2003. *The Pact: Three Young Men Make a Promise and Fulfill a Dream.* New York: Riverhead Trade.

Death and trauma materials. www.nassp.org.

DeCremer, D. 2001. "Effects of Roles and Performance Feedback on the Equality Rule in Resource-Sharing Tasks." *Journal of Social Psychology* 141, no. 1: 153.

"Divorce and How It Affects a Child." http://nh.essortment.com/divorcehoweffe_rhcq.htm.

"Effects of Divorce on Children." http://ut.essortment.com/effectsdivorce_rjqk.htm.

Ehrenreich, B. 2002. *Nickled and Dimed: On (Not) Getting By in America.* New York: Holt.

Etzioni, A. 1993.*The Spirit of Community: Rights, Responsibilities, and the Communitarian Agenda.* New York: Crown.

"Facts about Media Violence and Effects on the American Family." Baby Bag Online. www.babybag.com/articles/amaviol.htm.

Feelings, T. 1993. *Soul Looks Back in Wonder.* New York: Dial.

Feng, G., and English, J. 1974. *Chuang Tsu: Inner Chapters.* New York: Vintage.

Fields, J. M., and Smith, K. E. 1998. *Poverty, Family Structure, and Child Well-Being: Indicators from the SIPP.* Washington, D.C.: Population Division, U.S. Bureau of the Census. www.census.gov/population/www/documentation/twps0023.html.

First Amendment Center. 1999. *A Teacher's Guide to Religion in the Public Schools.* Publication no. FO2A. Nashville, TN: First Amendment Center.

Froschl, M., and Gropper, N. 1999. "Fostering Friendships, Curbing Bullying." *Educational Leadership* 56, no. 8: 72–75.

Goldberg, M. 2001 *Lessons from Exceptional School Leaders.* Alexandria, VA: Association for Supervision and Curriculum Development.

Grief Materials. www.griefwatch.com.

Haycock, K. 2001. "Closing the Achievement Gap." *Educational Leadership* 58, no. 6: 6–11.

Holloway, J. H. 2001. "Research Link/Inclusion and Students with Disabilities." *Educational Leadership* 58, no. 6: 86–88.

The Homeless Home Movie, review. www.2.bitstream.net/~mvisions (retrieved March 1, 2004).

Jackel, S. 1996. "Asperger's Syndrome: Educational Management Issues." www.ozemail.com.au/~prussia/asperger/teach.htm (retrieved March 16, 2003).

Jackson, K. 2000. *Family Homelessness*. New York: Taylor & Francis.

Johnson, S. 2002. *Who Moved My Cheese?* New York: Putnam.

Killingbeck, D. 2000. "The Role of Television News in the Construction of School Violence as a Moral Panic." *Journal of Criminal Justice Popular Culture* 8, no. 3: 186–202.

Kissinger, K. 1994. *All the Colors We Are*. St. Paul, MN: Redleaf.

Knafo, A. 2003. "Contexts, Relationship Quality, and Family Value Socialization: The Case of Parent–School Ideological Fit in Israel." *Personal Relationships* 10, no. 3: 371–89.

Kotulak, R. 2003. "Poverty Can Damage Children's Potential for Learning, Research Says." Knight Ridder/Tribune News Service, December 4, K4753.

Kozol, J. 1989. *Rachel and Her Children: Homeless Families in America*. New York: Fawcett.

———. 1992. *Savage Inequalities: Children in America's Schools*. New York: HarperCollins.

Kulber-Ross, Elisabeth. 1997. *On Death and Dying*. New York: Scribner.

Ladd, G. W. 1999. "Peer Relationships and Social Competence during Early and Middle Childhood." *Annual Review of Psychology*, 1–30. www.findarticles.com/cfdis/m0961/1999.Annual/544442303/print.jhtml (retrieved December 2003).

Lambda Legal Fund. www.lambdalegal.org.

Leach, F. 2003. "Learning to Be Violent: The Role of the School in Developing Adolescent Gendered Behavior." *Compare* 33, no. 3: 385–401.

Lee, E., Menkart, D., and Ozazawa-Rey, M. 1998. *Beyond Heroes and Holidays: A Practical K–12 Anti-racist, Multicultural Education and Professional Development*. Washington, D.C.: Network of Educators on the Americas.

Levine, A. 2003. "It's a Sin to Deny Kids a Quality Education." *Curriculum Review* 43, no. 4: 3–4.

Lipson, J., ed. 2001. *Hostile Hallways: Bullying, Teasing, and Sexual Harassment in School*. Washington, D.C.: AAUW Educational Foundation.

Lively, K. L., and Kleine, P. F. 1996. *School as a Tool for Survival for Homeless Children*. New York: Taylor & Francis.

London, V. 2001. *Lucy and the Liberty Quilt*. Frisco, TX: Sparklesoup Studios.

Loewen, J. W. 1995. *Lies My Teacher Told Me: Everything Your American History Textbook Got Wrong*. New York: New Press of the City University of New York.

McCain, B. C. 2001. *Nobody Knew What to Do: A Story about Bullying*. Morton Grove, IL: Albert Whitman & Co.

McKendrick, J. 2004. "Deep Impact (Effect of Poverty on Children)." *Community Care*, 24.

McKenzie K. J., and Crowcroft, N. A. 1994. "Race, Ethnicity, Culture, and Science: Researchers Should Understand and Justify Their Use of Ethnic Groupings." *British Medical Journal* 309, no. 6950: 286–88.

McNamara, D. 2002. "Reaction to Traumatic Events Tied to Patient's Age. When Is It PTSD?" *Pediatric News* 36, no. 9: 34–35.

Metzger, J. 1995. *Kids Count on Families: A Special Report on the State of Our Families*. ERIC Document Reproduction Services, no. ED 422084.

Meyerhoff, M. K. 1999. "Peer Pressure Protection." *Pediatrics for Parents* 18, no. 7: 8.

Nathanson, A. I. 2001. "Parents versus Peers: Exploring the Significance of Peer Mediation of Antisocial Television." *Communication Research* 28, no. 3: 251–75.

National Center for Post-Traumatic Stress Disorder. www.ncptsd.org.

National Council on Alcoholism, 12 West 21st St., New York, NY 10010 (212-206-6770).

National Parent Teacher Association. www.pta.org.

Nieto, S. M. 2002–2003. "Profoundly Multicultural Questions." *Educational Leadership* 60, no. 9: 6–10.

Paige, R. 2003a. *Guidance on Constitutionally Protected Prayer in Public Elementary and Secondary Schools*. www.ed.gov/inits/religionandschools/prayer_guidance.html (retrieved December 2003).

Paige, R. 2003b. *Secretary's Letter on Constitutionally Protected Prayer in Public Elementary and Secondary Schools*. www.ed.gov/inits/religionandschools/letter_030207.html (retrieved December 2003).

Parents without Partners. www.parentswithoutpartners.org.

Payne, R. 1995. *Framework for Working with Students and Adults from Poverty*. Highlands, TX: aha! Process.

Peer pressure information and materials. www.scholastic.com/schoolage/grade5/development/5_copingpeerpress.htm.

Perlmutter, P. 2000. "Double Standards, Double Talk, and Multiple Troubles." *Independent Review* 5, no. 2: 313.

Piper, M. 1996. *And Jill Came Tumbling After.* Morristown, FL: Ritamelia.

Preboth, M. 2000. "Effects of Mass Media Exposure in Children." *American Family Physician* 61, no. 3: 890.

Raban, B., and Ure, C. 1999. *Literacy in the Preschool*. ERIC Reproduction Service, no. ED 445317. www.eduref.org.

Race, culture, and ethnicity in education is covered extensively in the Harvard University Fellows program on the same topic. www.gse.harvard.edu/news/features/postdoc09012001.html.

Schilbrack, K. 2003. "Religious Diversity and the Closed Mind." *Journal of Religion* 83, no. 1: 100–108.

Schlozman, S. C. 2002a. "The Shrink in the Classroom: Fighting School Violence." *Educational Leadership* 60, no. 2: 89–90.

———. 2002b. "The Shrink in the Classroom: When Illness Strikes." *Educational Leadership* 60, 1: 82–83.

———. 2002c. "The Shrink in the Classroom: When 'Just Say No' Isn't Enough." *Educational Leadership* 59, no. 7: 87–89.

Schniedewinde, N., and Davidson, E. 1998. *Open Minds to Equality: A Sourcebook of Learning Activities to Affirm Diversity and Promote Equality.* 2nd ed. Boston: Allyn & Bacon.

Sewell, G. T. 1999. "Religion Comes to School." *Phi Delta Kappan* 81, no. 1: 10–16.

Shannon, D. 2000. *The Rain Came Down.* New York: Blue Sky.

Shellard, E. 2002. *Recognizing and Preventing Bullying.* Arlington, VA: Educational Research Service.

Shields, C. M. 2000. "Learning from Difference: Considerations for Schools as Communities." *Curriculum Inquiry* 30, no. 3: 275–95.

Stone, D. 1988. *Policy, Paradox, and Political Reason.* New York: Scott, Foresman.

Tarpley, N. A. 1994. *Testimony: Young African-Americans on Self-Discovery and Black Identity.* Boston: Beacon.

Thorp, C. 2002–2003. "Web Wonders/Equity and Opportunity." *Educational Leadership* 60, no. 4: 96.

Walker, L. S., Garber, J., Smith, C., VanSlyke, D. A., and Claar, R. L. 2001. "The Relation of Daily Stressors to Somatic and Emotional Symptoms in Children with and without Recurrent Abdominal Pain." *Journal of Consulting Clinical Psychology* 69: 85–91.

Wessler, S., and Preble, W. 2003. *The Respectful School: How Educators and Students Can Conquer Hate and Harassment.* Alexandria, VA: Association for Supervision and Curriculum Development.

REFERENCES

Carter, S. C. 2000. *No Excuses: Lessons from 21 High-Performing, High-Poverty Schools.* Washington, D.C.: Heritage Foundation.

Glickman, C. D., Gordon, S., and Ross-Gordon, J. M. 2003. *SuperVision and Instructional Leadership: A Developmental Approach.* 6th ed. Boston: Allyn & Bacon.

Goodlad, J. 1984. *A Place Called School.* Orlando, FL: McGraw-Hill.

Guba, E. G., and Lincoln, Y. S. 1989. *Fourth Generation Evaluation.* Newbury Park, CA: Sage.

Guskey, T. R. 1999. *Evaluating Professional Development.* Vol. 1. Newbury Park, CA: Sage.

Hebert, E. A. 1999. "Rugtime for Teachers: Reinventing the Faculty Meeting." *Phi Delta Kappan* 81, no. 3: 219–22.

Huling, L., and Resta, V. 2001. "Teacher Mentoring as Professional Development." *ERIC Digest.* Washington, D.C.: AACTE.

Klein, M. W. 1997. *The American Street Gang: Its Nature, Prevalence, and Control.* New York: Oxford University Press.

Kulber-Ross, Elisabeth. 1997. *On Death and Dying.* New York: Scribner.

Merriam-Webster's Online Dictionary. www.m-w.com/cgi-bin/dictionary?book=Dictionary&va=conundrum.

National Survey on Drug Use and Health. 2002. http://oas.samhsa.gov/nhsda.htm.

Office of Applied Statistics [SAMHSA]. 2004. www.oas.samhsa.gov.

Pelifian, H. 2002. "Largest Education Budget in the World Failing American Schools." www.toogoodreports.com/column/general/pelifian/20021201-tfss .htm.

Schlozman, S. C. 2002. "The Shrink in the Classroom: Why 'Just Say No' Isn't Enough." *Educational Leadership* 59, no. 7: 87–89.

Tomlinson, C. A. 2001. *How to Differentiate Instruction in Mixed-Ability Classrooms.* 2nd ed. Alexandria, VA: Association for Supervision and Curriculum Development.

INDEX

ABOUT THE AUTHORS

Jacque and Julie are passionate believers in the power of good that teachers and administrators can bring to the learning environment of children and young people in our world. The ever-changing dynamics of American society make it imperative that we take the time to discuss our roles and responsibilities in supporting positive change. We hope that this book will help promote the dialogue.

When she is not teaching or writing, Jacque is actively involved in the lives of her three daughters and her three grandchildren. What an inspiration each are.

When she is not writing with Jacque, Julie is reading with her two children.

You can reach them at:
Jacque: jjacobs@wcu.edu
Julie: jrotholz@gwm.sc.edu